Fairy Tale
Interrupted

Fairy Tale Interrupted

A MEMOIR OF LIFE, LOVE, AND LOSS

RoseMarie Terenzio

GALLERY BOOKS

New York   London   Toronto   Sydney   New Delhi

Gallery Books
A Division of Simon & Schuster, Inc.
1230 Avenue of the Americas
New York, NY 10020

NOTE TO READERS
Certain names and identifying characteristics have been changed.

First Gallery Books hardcover edition January 2012

GALLERY BOOKS and colophon are registered trademarks of Simon & Schuster, Inc.

For information about special discounts for bulk purchases,
please contact Simon & Schuster Special Sales at 1-866-506-1949
or business@simonandschuster.com.

The Simon & Schuster Speakers Bureau can bring authors
to your live event. For more information or to book an event,
contact the Simon & Schuster Speakers Bureau at 1-866-248-3049
or visit our website at www.simonspeakers.com.

Designed by Davina Mock-Maniscalco

Manufactured in the United States of America

10   9   8   7   6   5   4   3   2   1

Library of Congress Cataloging-in-Publication Data

Terenzio, RoseMarie.
  Fairy tale interrupted : a memoir of life, love, and
loss / RoseMarie Terenzio.—1st Gallery Books hardcover ed.
      p. cm.
  1. Kennedy, John F. (John Fitzgerald), 1960–1999. 2. Kennedy, John F.
(John Fitzgerald), 1960–1999—Friends and associates. 3. Terenzio, RoseMarie.
4. Bronx (New York, N.Y.)—Biography. I. Title.
  E843.K42T47 2011
  973.922092—dc23
  [B]
                                    2011034344

ISBN 978-1-4391-8767-8
ISBN 978-1-4391-8769-2 (ebook)

For Marion and Anthony Terenzio
With love, admiration, and gratitude.
You gave me everything I need and made me the best I could be.

For Frank Giordano
I had the time of my life and I owe it all to you.

For John Kennedy
With gratitude for your generosity, wisdom, and encouragement,
and for giving me the opportunity of a lifetime.

For Carolyn Bessette Kennedy
Thank you for your strength, kindness, wit, and friendship.

For Rita Leanza
My godmother, my friend, and my confidante.

There goes my hero.
He's ordinary.

—"My Hero," Foo Fighters

PROLOGUE

The office was quiet when I got in around nine o'clock. Too bad it wouldn't stay that way for long. Once John arrived, it would be nonstop until he got on the plane for his trip to Italy.

I had an hour to organize myself before I spent the rest of the day organizing him. I checked his voice mail—the first thing I did every single morning for the five years I worked for John— and he'd received six new messages since I left the office at nine the night before. Not bad; definitely not as bad as it could get. I wrote them all down (except for the two from John, asking me to remind him of things he had to do) on message slips, which I piled up and left in a slot on my desk for him to read on his own time. I never bombarded John with information as soon as he walked in the door. He had a very calm demeanor—panic was not his style.

Instead, after a simple greeting of "Morning" when he arrived and walked past my desk, I always gave him a minute to sit in his office and get settled, and I waited for him to call me.

"Rosie?" he yelled only a few minutes later.

"Coming," I said, rising from my chair and grabbing his calendar, a pen, and a legal pad.

I found him going through the stack of mail that I had covered in sticky notes with various instructions or questions. The whole of Central Park and the Upper West Side skyline was his backdrop as I sat across from him and the office's wall of windows.

I started in on his day: an editorial meeting at noon; lunch immediately after at Limoncello with Jeff Sachs, his friend and the executive director of Reaching Up, the charity they cofounded; then a 3:00 p.m. meeting with Biz Mitchell, executive editor of John's magazine, *George*.

"Oh, brother, Rosie. You are going to have a miserable day if you don't find some time in that calendar for me to work out," he said.

So it was going to be like that today.

Whenever John was preparing to leave for a trip abroad, the atmosphere in the office was more hectic than usual, with me double-checking all the travel arrangements, getting vital answers on layouts and story ideas for editors before he was out of touch, and amassing absolutely everything he needed to have in his hands before taking off. That was on top of the regular load of phone calls, meetings, and mail. I detected a note of tension in his voice and knew he needed to release it at the gym. As I was his assistant, the more frazzled he got, the calmer I had to be.

"Okay. I'll find you forty-five minutes for the gym. You also have to write that thank-you note to Paul Begala today."

"No problem," he answered, already distracted and squeezing his stress ball.

When I got back to my desk, another eight voice mail messages were waiting for me, and the phones were going crazy, as they would until about seven that night. I was so used to the ringing, I almost didn't hear it anymore. I did hear the thud of the box of John's mail delivered to my desk. *Forget it.* That would have to wait till tomorrow when he was gone.

Among the new messages were a bunch that had to do with the upcoming auction of his mother's estate: Reporters from the *New York Times,* the *Daily News,* and *Time* called looking for quotes. And Taylor, the woman handling the auction at Sotheby's, left a terse "Please have John call me back." I knew from her tone that she needed to discuss something important.

I actually didn't know anything about the auction, except what was announced to the public: Sotheby's was selling many items from Jackie Onassis's estate the following week. From the minute it was announced, I got the vibe from John that he didn't want it to take up much of his time. He refused to give me any details and dragged his feet when he had to do something for it. (I suspected his trip to Italy was perfectly timed to miss the event.) While John acted as if the auction was not a priority, I was fielding numerous calls and requests—not just from the media but from people wanting to attend the event or get a catalog—yet I didn't have any information. I didn't even know that the brown paper shopping bag he asked me to take to the house of his sister, Caroline, the week before had been filled with $2 million worth of jewelry. If I had, I would have killed him. John just wanted it to be over, so I had to figure out how to handle it without asking too many annoying questions. I acted like I knew what I was doing; pretending I had been there before was my specialty.

The mad dash to get John out of the office on time began as soon as he returned that afternoon from his abbreviated workout. There were new phone messages that I had to discuss with him. ("Is Carolyn also going to that dinner with Leonard Lauder?" "No, it's just work." "The Robin Hood Foundation wants you to speak at the next board meeting." "Okay, just put it on the calendar and write up some notes.")

And the auction again.

"Taylor called a few more times," I said. "So did your sister."

"Okay."

"Are you going to call them back?"

"I said *I'll call.*"

That was John not dealing with it, I could tell. I wished he'd either tell me what to do or call back, but I couldn't push him any more unless I wanted my head taken off.

"Here's the stationery and a pen to write Paul's thank-you note," I said, putting both on his desk. "It has to go out *today.*"

I walked out of his office and went to the bathroom to cool off. We were together almost all day, every day. And working for John opened doors to places I never imagined I'd ever enter, like the hottest clubs in town, the most coveted events, exclusive restaurants, even his house in Hyannis, which he lent me for a week every summer. Carolyn, his wife, and I spoke on the phone about a hundred times a day and often hung out after work to talk about boys, clothes, and the latest celebrity gossip. John and I were as close as family, and like family, we got on each other's nerves.

When I returned, John's office was empty. He had a lot to do, so where was he? I walked a short way down the hallway.

He was in the office of *George*'s publisher, Michael Berman, chitchatting.

"John, what are you doing?"

"Shut up, Rosie. Stop nagging."

We were both frustrated, but he got up and returned to his office to write his thank-you note, return his last calls, and reply to editors' story ideas.

Finally, it was five o'clock: time to get him into the car and out of my hair.

"Car's downstairs, John," I shouted from my chair.

Five minutes went by with no response, so I walked into his office and said, "You have to go *now*." He nodded and started to stand up when Michael walked in to tell him a funny story about his run-in with the publisher of *Esquire*. "Michael! John has to go," I pleaded, but they both ignored me and Michael finished his story.

It took another twenty minutes to get John downstairs, because people stopped him everywhere: in the hallway, in the elevator, even in the bathroom. Finally, sweet Jesus, we made it outside.

On the way to the car, a couple of construction workers spotted John and called out to him, as people always did when they saw him in public. (When I first met John, one morning I saw him on the street as I walked to work and shouted his name, but he didn't turn to acknowledge me. Later, I confronted him and asked why he had been so rude. "Rosie, do you know how many people yell 'John' when I'm walking down the street? If I turned to every one of them, I'd never get to work.")

"Hey, John-John, I like your magazine!" one of the construction guys yelled.

"Thanks, but it's one John," he said.

I handed him a folder that held absolutely everything he needed: his itinerary, a contact list, stories to edit, stories to review, pages to show the ad people, and more.

"Do you have your passport and wallet?" I asked.

He patted his pocket to double-check.

"John, one more thing. I'm getting a lot of calls about the auction. What should I tell people about that?"

He shot me a look. "How should I know? Do I look like I work at Sotheby's?"

Dick! He was lucky he got in that car, or else I would have choked him. *Thanks a lot, John,* I thought as the Town Car rode away.

I bought some Camel Lights and packed them into my hand as I walked down the hallway to creative director Matt Berman's office, which doubled as the magazine's rec room. The office had every new magazine, ashtrays, Diet Coke, and a sofa—all the makings of a good lounge. That's where Carolyn hung out whenever she visited, not in John's office. She'd flop down on the couch, a whirlwind of handbags and stories, and spend hours leafing through magazines and smoking, so that by the time she left, Matt's office looked like a nightclub. Now it was my turn on the couch.

"I could hear you pounding on those cigarettes from in here," Matt said. "Bad day?"

"You don't know the half of it," I said, taking a drag and a sip of Diet Coke. Once John was gone, a Coke and a cigarette on Matt's couch was my ritual. Matt used to say he always knew when John had left for the day because he heard the can open in his office.

We weren't supposed to smoke in the office. But it was *George*. We could get away with almost anything. If we'd set the curtains on fire, the publishing company would have said, "Okay, just put them out when you're done."

I bitched to Matt about John's insensitivity, stubbornness, and a litany of other complaints. But truthfully, I was in heaven. With John on a plane for the next seven hours, I had something that was very rare for me—an evening all to myself. Not only could I actually leave the office by 7:00 p.m., I also wouldn't have to worry about misplaced keys, last-minute letters to celebrities for requests to pose for the magazine cover, reporters on deadlines, people wanting RSVPs, or any of the other details I dealt with day and night.

I planned to enjoy it, and that meant going home, ordering in, and zoning out in front of the television. Heaven.

The buzzer rang with my food (interrupting a rerun of *My So-Called Life*), and reaching inside my bag for my wallet, I found a white envelope with my name on it. It was in John's handwriting. I instantly pulled open the envelope. Inside, I counted ten hundred-dollar bills—a thousand dollars in cash.

Holy shit.

Was he kidding me? I read the accompanying note.

The money was awesome, but the note was even better. I had no way of knowing how to handle an auction, and I felt as though he didn't get that. But of course, he wound up acknowledging it with the most thoughtful, low-key, classy thank-you I could ever imagine receiving. Even when we

JOHN KENNEDY

Roe

This means you
have to commid
crimes if I ask
you to.
    Don't get used to it
we only auction Mummy's
jewelry once a life.
Thanks love, JK
baby.
        Enjoy!

1633 Broadway, 41st Fl., New York, NY 10019

bickered, John knew I appreciated everything he did for me and that I always had his back.

John's life and my life were intertwined in many ways. Working for him, I was his gatekeeper, controlling access to someone whom everyone wanted time with. I protected him and his time from people and things that weren't in his best interest. As a friend, my role wasn't all that different, except that I made him laugh. He teased me ruthlessly, and I gave it right back to him. He loved that I treated him like a normal person and not like JFK Jr. As his loyal assistant and friend, I would have done anything for him. Even though I never expected anything more than a paycheck, John gave me opportunities that changed my life forever, taking me on the most dramatic journey a girl in New York City could ever dream of. Especially a girl like me.

CHAPTER

1

—

Two types of people exist in this world: those who are obsessed with the Kennedys and those who aren't. My big Italian family from the Bronx sat squarely in the latter camp. My dad, a staunch Republican, had no patience for the family synonymous with the Democratic Party. And my mom was too busy to care about politics on any side of the aisle at all.

Obviously, I understood why it created a major stir when John F. Kennedy Jr. first started calling the offices of the Manhattan public relations firm where I worked, PR/NY, but it didn't give me the same thrill as it did Liz, the office manager, and Tricia, the receptionist, who would giggle and exchange meaningful glances whenever he was on the line. To me John was just a political type; I would have been more interested in meeting his celebrity girlfriend Daryl Hannah.

It was funny to see Liz and Tricia get excited about anything. The two pretty hipsters shared a blasé attitude toward most aspects of life, including work. But I saw a hint of triumph on the face of whoever got to shout "John's on the phone" to Michael Berman, cofounder of the firm and the man who gave me the best job I'd ever had.

Michael started PR/NY after convincing his partner, Will Steere—whom he met while both were at the big international PR firm Burson-Marsteller—to take a chunk of Burson's business and go out on their own. During my interview in the office, decorated with that brand of sleek minimalism that makes you feel fat and poor, I thought, *I'm definitely not sophisticated enough for this*. But Michael was able to get past my outer-borough accent—and my outfit, a red pleated skirt and black-and-white polka-dot blouse that made me look as if someone threw me into a sales rack at Strawberry, spun me around, and set me loose.

Working at PR/NY was so different from my last job as a junior-level publicist at a midtown PR company that mainly worked with book publishers, where our offices were small and dingy and the big perk was getting to charge ten dollars a week at the local deli. Will and Michael, meanwhile, were young, rich, and good-looking.

Michael, in his jeans, nice shirts, and ever-present tan, ate at Nobu, ran with a celebrity crowd, and dated a well-known interior decorator. Michael could talk to anyone about anything, and he drove the business aspect of PR/NY because he was great at strategy. I worked harder than anyone else in the office to prove to him that I belonged there, that he hadn't made a mistake in taking a chance on me. If Will needed me to run an errand, I was on it. When Michael told me to revise a press release twenty times, I did it without attitude.

So when JFK Jr. called the office, to me it was no different from Christopher Reeve or any other celebrity calling for Michael. Other than enjoying watching Liz and Tricia get silly at the sound of his voice, I didn't give him much thought until the day he unexpectedly arrived at PR/NY.

Without knowing who was waiting, I buzzed him in, as I always did when someone rang the bell, and punched in the code to open the door. But as I tugged on the handle, he was pulling on the other side, so neither of us could open it. We both released the door, and I reentered the code, then stood back and waited for the person to open the door. Nothing. *Oh God,* I thought. *This isn't that complicated.* I punched in the code one more time and pulled, just as he decided to pull yet again.

"You have to let go of the knob," I said, getting more frustrated.

"Sorry," came the muted reply.

Once again I entered the code and was finally able to open the door, discovering to my horror that I had just snapped at John F. Kennedy Jr.

"Hi," he said casually.

"Hi."

He was much better looking in person than in any photograph of him I'd ever seen—and he didn't exactly photograph poorly. Wearing a court-jester-type knit hat, John was accompanied by a large, drooling German shepherd that looked sad and not too friendly.

"Is Michael here?" John asked. Although I felt like dying, I pulled myself together and walked John inside. The previous summer, John had left the assistant district attorney position he'd held for four years, and he first started coming into the PR/NY office about once a week, and then every other day, sometimes more. By the spring of 1994, it was as if he and his slightly demented rescue dog, Sam, worked at PR/NY— only none of the staff, except for Michael, knew what he was doing there. Even Will had no idea. But you didn't ask Michael anything, even if you co-owned the company. Discretion was his stock-in-trade.

Will was a dyed-in-the-wool Republican raised in the wealthy Connecticut town of Darien, and every day he wore a perfect suit and a different Hermès tie, which stood out against the low-key vibe in the office. One of my first days on the job, I asked him if he had an important client meeting. He looked at me like he didn't understand the question, as if that were the only proper way to dress.

Will seemed to feel it was his political duty to get a rise out of John, and he loved to greet John with a condescending "Hey, Junior!" anytime he walked in the door. John refused to take the bait, and instead nodded hello and headed into the conference room with Michael.

Because Michael and John were both on the board of Naked Angels—a nonprofit theater company in New York supported by celebrities such as Marisa Tomei and Sarah Jessica Parker—Liz, Tricia, and I decided the most obvious explanation for their meetings was that they were planning a fund-raiser. But their conversations often became heated; we'd see John gesticulating wildly, water bottle in hand, through the slightly open door. And they were always careful to collect the papers spread across the big wooden table before they left the conference room. I was as curious as the next person but figured John was none of my business. That is, until he made himself my business.

A few months after John had become a regular at the office, I came into work one morning really hurting. The night before, I'd made the mistake of drinking free cocktails at a launch party for a start-up company that delivered anything—movies, condoms, ice cream—to your apartment day or night. As usual, Frank was along for the ride.

I met Frank Giordano, my soul mate, in college, where it was love at first sight. I was walking out of the cafeteria when I spotted a gorgeous guy—six foot two, thick hair, dark-brown eyes—wearing all white and propped against a yellow Riviera. Frank knew the effect his stunning appearance had on people and often used it, almost comically, to his advantage. With him, nothing was off-limits.

We connected instantly, and from that moment on, we were completely inseparable. We did everything together, except have sex. I had never met anyone like him: gorgeous, charismatic, a sweet soul. Hardly ever in a bad mood, Frank was always on a mission to make sure everyone around him was having a good time. After college, I moved with Frank into his mother's home, a gigantic house in Bronxville, New York, until I got the call every New Yorker dreams about, one asking if I'd be interested in a rent-stabilized apartment. Frank convinced me to take the place (he wasn't only my best friend and confidant but also my real estate broker) even though it was the most vile, dank, dark three hundred square feet of grime I had ever seen. He promised he would transform the place for me, and he did, stripping and bleaching the floors and repainting. By the time I moved in, the walls were a crisp white and the wood floor felt smooth beneath my feet. There was a little kitchen, a built-in bookcase, a bed, and a bathroom—all for me.

I had no idea what to do with all this privacy. Growing up in a two-story house on Garfield Street crammed with my mom, dad, great-grandmother, grandma, older sisters Anita, Andrea, and Amy, and two dogs, I wasn't used to alone time. Someone was always in the bathroom, on the couch, or in front of the fridge. Outside wasn't much better, with neighbors hanging out their windows and screaming at one another.

But Frank didn't give me a chance to feel lonely. As soon as the apartment was ready, he called all our friends and told them to come over to my new place. I cranked the stereo that Michael and Will had bought me as a housewarming gift and poured everyone drinks before we headed out for a night of dancing at Rouge. When we called it quits around 4:00 a.m., I didn't have to wait for a train at Grand Central or have Frank drive me home. We just hopped in a cab and within minutes were in my new apartment. As far as I was concerned, I had arrived.

Frank, always my first call in the morning and last call at night, loved my new life even more than I did. He came as my date to many events, like the launch party for the Manhattan delivery service, where we drank several Speedy Deliveries, the party's signature cocktail, and ended up at a gay bar drinking margaritas.

After mixing way too much booze, the next morning I tried in vain to settle my queasy stomach and pounding head with a large coffee from the cart outside the office building. Wearing a pair of extra-large sunglasses, I could smell the alcohol wafting from my pores. The worst part: it was only Monday. (Frank and I loved going out on Sunday nights, because that's when people who lived in the city went out.) I couldn't imagine getting through the morning, let alone the week.

All I wanted to do was get into the cozy confines of my office and hide out for the rest of the day. My love affair with my office had started the minute I arrived at PR/NY. The view was of the building's air shaft, but its location at the back of the building gave it a snug quality, where a girl could feel safe calling her friends to bitch about bad dates, have a good cry when she lost a client or, like this morning, nurse a particularly bruising hangover.

As I passed through reception, the light streaming in the windows and bouncing off the white walls felt downright debilitating. Making a beeline for my office, I kept my sunglasses on and held on to my coffee as if it were a life raft. I relaxed a bit at the thought of momentarily resting my head on my desk, and opened the door to my cozy little office.

What the . . . ?

John and a man I didn't recognize were piling my possessions into a cardboard moving box. Adrenaline surged through my body, instantly curing my hangover. No longer weary or nauseous, I was mad—and confused.

"Oh, hey—" John said.

"Excuse me," I said, cutting him off. "What are you doing? And who are *you*?" I pointed at the handsome, silver-haired man in jeans and a fitted T-shirt who was wielding an industrial vacuum cleaner like a pro.

"This is Effie. He works for me and my family, helping with—"

"Why is he touching my stuff?"

I whipped off my sunglasses and got into a staring match with Effie.

"Michael said it was okay for me to move in here," John said.

"Well, it's not okay," I said, spinning around to address him directly. That's when I noticed that not only had they taken down my bulletin board without asking but, in the process, they had ripped one of my most treasured possessions: my Howard Stern head shot. I was crushed.

I thought Howard was a god. I admired how he disguised intelligent dialogue about political and social issues as a radio show about farts and strippers. Plus, he made me laugh out loud every single morning. Brilliant, unpretentious, and funny, Howard spoke my language. And anyone who knew me knew I loved him. That's why a colleague from my old job asked his friend, a producer at K-Rock, where Howard did his show, for the irreplaceable head shot, which was now ruined.

"We can figure this out," John said.

"*Figure this out?* Clearly *we're* not figuring out anything, because *you* have already packed everything up," I said.

"I'm sure we can find some sort of solution," he said.

"I don't know why you need an office, anyway. You don't even have a job."

"Michael!" John said loudly.

"Maybe you get away with this everywhere else you go, but not here."

"Michael!"

Despite my show of bravado, insecurity welled up inside me at the realization that somebody more important could just walk in and take everything away from me—my amazing office, job, and new life in Manhattan. I should have been prepared for this. But I wasn't ready for defeat.

Michael shouted for me to get into his office. I left John and his butler boxing up my life and slowly took the ten steps to Michael's office. This was serious. No one ever went in there except to have their review. He was the kind of boss who left you alone. He always had your back, even if a client was unhappy, but he wasn't a micromanager. Instead, he taught by example about what worked and what didn't in PR.

What the hell had I been thinking, telling off John F. Kennedy Jr.? Was I insane? *Oh well,* I thought. *My time at PR/NY was fun while it lasted. . . . Starbucks, here I come.*

I stepped into Michael's immaculate office. He sat behind his sleek desk, with all his perfect pens arranged in an elegant leather cup and a box of wheat grass placed neatly in the corner. His hands were clasped in front of him, and he had a big smirk on his face. He wasn't angry; in fact, he seemed to be thoroughly enjoying the drama. Michael never kissed John's ass and was apparently pleased to see someone following his example.

"You know, Rose," Michael said, amused. "You could be arrested in some states for the way you just spoke to him."

"Why is he taking my office?" I whined.

"He's working with me now. Let's be realistic. You really think I'm going to give him the smaller office? You're going to be just fine. What he's doing isn't infringing on your turf. In fact, it has nothing to do with you. So let's get on with it."

I got the message and left his office, grateful to still have my job. Even though Michael had found my outburst funny, I knew I had to keep my Italian temper in check, since it could get me in a lot of trouble. If I got into a fight with a guy I was dating,

I had no problem walking out and leaving him in a restaurant. If I didn't like what somebody was saying to me on the phone, I hung up. During one particularly heated fight with Frank at his apartment, I pulled everything he owned off his bookshelves and dumped a garbage bag of clothes he'd left at my house in a heap on the floor. I don't remember exactly what triggered the blowup, but I ransacked his place; it looked like a crime scene when I was done with it.

My anger issues were the by-product of a tense childhood in a chaotic environment that was ready to explode at any moment. And the woman holding the lighter to the powder keg was Marion, my Sicilian mother. Talk about an Italian temper.

My mother was usually working two jobs, carrying the family's financial load while trying to raise four kids in direct opposition to the way she was raised. My grandparents were not exactly stellar parents, and when they split up, my mother was bounced around like the kid no one wanted. She was determined to do a better job with her kids, and that was a huge amount of pressure. My sisters, Anita, Andrea, and Amy, are older than me by seventeen, ten, and four years, respectively; they helped raise me and were always much better at dealing with our explosive household than I was.

When I was six years old, I made the mistake of complaining about my Christmas gifts. I had actually received something I loved, a doll that blinked her eyes when I moved her. My aunt Rita always bought me a doll for Christmas because she knew how much I loved them. My other gifts were all practical— socks, sweaters, shoes—so the baby was my big present. But the day after Christmas is always a major comedown, and like many kids, I was poised for a meltdown when I dragged myself and my new doll into the kitchen and announced that I had nothing to play with. I whined and cried until my mom eventually had enough. She put down her cup of black coffee and took a deep pull on her Kool cigarette.

"Enough already!" she yelled, then snatched the doll from my hands and slammed it against the wall, shattering its torso, twisting its limbs, and sending the blinking eyes into a permanently cockeyed stare. And then she threw the mangled body at me as I wept and begged her to stop.

"If you don't stop, I'll really give you something to cry about," she threatened.

On another occasion, my mom had spent all day Saturday cleaning and had left my room in immaculate condition. Two days later, she came in to find the floor littered with clothes, the bed unmade, and books and papers scattered everywhere. She was silent, which was a lot scarier than her yelling, and then she began snatching T-shirts, jeans, and sweaters from the floor and tossing them into my doll's crib. I watched as my mother pulled the crib over to the window, lifted the screen, and dumped the contents onto the front porch. For a moment, I thought I'd be next. But my mom walked out of the room without a glance in my direction. Racing downstairs, I grabbed a garbage bag and headed out to collect my stuff, humiliated, as a small group of neighbors who had already gathered to check out the action stared at me. The people on our block liked nothing better than a little domestic disturbance.

The main source of frustration in our home revolved around us never having enough money. Between the two of them, my parents always seemed to have ten jobs. Secretarial work was Mom's mainstay, but she also cleaned doctors' offices and worked at a perfume factory in the Bronx where fragrances such as Charlie and Jontue were manufactured. Her winter coat reeked of those scents. My dad sometimes cleaned offices with her. He also worked in a liquor store during the day and as a bartender at night.

Despite all the jobs, we never had two dimes to rub together. If the car broke down, we could either get a new transmission or pay the electric bill; if tuition was due, we could either pay for school or pay the phone bill; if the boiler broke when we were low on cash, we went without heat. Those trade-offs were the one constant in my childhood.

My father, Anthony, worked every bit as hard as my mother; he saw himself as something of an entrepreneur, but his businesses were not successful. He opened a deli that went bust because his partner walked out; a pizza place that went bankrupt, leaving my parents buried under a fifty-thousand-dollar debt; and a candy shop on the corner, which also sold cigarettes and newspapers, that he had to shutter.

My mother, the breadwinner for most of our lives, became extremely anxious in the face of money problems. The financial burden was all on her shoulders—she was responsible for the family and she knew it. When she felt trapped, she lashed out. And with a husband who wasn't making enough to support four daughters, let alone reduce a mountain of debt, she always felt trapped.

Despite feeling trapped, my mother was fearless. Once, even the Catholic Church made it onto my mom's shit list. I was in the third grade at St. Dominic's, the Catholic school attended by generations of my family for over sixty years. The school had implemented a new policy that if your family didn't pay your tuition on time, you didn't get your report card. Up until then, the shame of not getting that little yellow card had been reserved for kids who failed a class. And that had never been me. But after overhearing the screaming matches between my parents about tuition checks, I knew I was a candidate for embarrassment that term. So there I was in class, shitting my pants as Sister Mary Josephine slowly worked her way through the alphabet, calling kids up one by one to claim their report cards. I felt the hard-backed wooden chair pressing into my spine as she reached the *R*'s, then the *S*'s, before intoning in her liturgical voice all the names beginning with *T*. No Terenzio. As soon as the bell rang, I raced out of that room, past my concerned friends, and ran the three blocks to my house.

When my mom got home from work later that night, the first thing she saw was my tear-streaked face.

"What happened?" she asked.

I told her about the humiliating report-card incident.

"How dare they? After I've put four kids through that school!" she screamed. "Your father's whole family went there, too. They should be ashamed of themselves." She lit a cigarette and blew smoke from her nostrils. "I'm going to let them know what I think of their Christian spirit."

My mother called the rectory the next morning and demanded to speak to the bishop, to whom she calmly explained the circumstances. "We're having a hard time, Bishop, but you know you'll get the money. I've put four kids through the school, and I hope you'll make an exception."

"I'm sorry, Mrs. Terenzio. This is the policy and it applies to everyone."

Wow. He clearly had no idea who he was dealing with:

Marion Terenzio did not mess around. She told him exactly what she thought of his Christian spirit and slammed the phone down.

That Sunday, we went to mass at St. Dominic's, as always. When I was a kid, that little sand-colored brick church, with its spire, heavy stained-glass windows, and dark interior, had all the majesty of a real cathedral; it seemed like St. Patrick's to me. Although, in truth, it was a small neighborhood church in a devout blue-collar outpost.

The mass on that particular Sunday was dedicated to celebrating the arrival of our new bishop, the same man responsible for the new "no tuition, no grades" policy. Beforehand, the bishop stood in the church vestibule, decked out in his pink-and-gold habiliments and smiling benevolently. With my father and sisters and me in tow, my mother tried to blow past him without a word, but the bishop stopped her.

"Good morning, Mrs. Terenzio," he said, putting his ring out for her to kiss. With a crowd of congregants gathered behind her in the receiving line, my mother shot the clergyman a look of utter disdain.

"Bishop," she said evenly, "you can kiss my ass before I'll kiss that ring."

She then marched us to the front of the church, where she prayed before God and the bishop without a shred of guilt or remorse.

My report card was waiting for me at school on Monday morning.

Twenty years later, on the heels of my own holier-than-thou battle with John, I decided to follow my mom's example and ignore him. John may have won my office, and I may have had to put up with him at work, but that didn't mean I had to like him or even acknowledge his existence.

It took a while for the guy who got whatever he wanted to take a hint. Every day, he would walk or Rollerblade past my office, greeting me with a cheerful "Good morning." And every day, I refused to respond or even make eye contact with him. I'd hear him coming, and just before he popped his head in to say hello, I would quickly pick up the receiver and pretend to be on the phone, thinking, *Fuck you. Have fun in your new office, buddy.*

I know it seems immature to be that rude to any coworker, let alone to John Kennedy, but it was a matter of pride. When I feel slighted, I don't back down. As it turned out, John was the same way—although his approach was very different. He said his chipper hellos each morning, seemingly oblivious to my ignoring him. John couldn't relax his perfect manners: they had been instilled in him at a very early age, just as my tough exterior had been. So the standoff went on for weeks.

During that time, John settled in to PR/NY, though none of us had any idea what he was doing there. He brought in an intern, a daughter of a family friend, to answer his phone and open his mail. She clearly had a crush on him and decided to bond with Sam, as if that unstable dog might be the way to John's heart. One day she was lying on the floor with Sam—yes, rolling around the office floor with a scary dog that snapped from time to time—and he bit her face. She refused to go to the hospital. Blood, rabies, whatever, Sam was John's dog, so it was all fine and good, just a scratch, nothing to worry about. . . . People were insane around John.

He was making me insane, too, and not just because he stole my office. The fact that we still didn't know what he was doing there began to worry me. After several months of his being there, it was obvious he couldn't be working on a charity event. And he couldn't just be renting office space—the place was nice but not *that* nice. Plus, Michael was distracted from the agency's day-to-day work—he didn't give my press releases the attention he once had or ask about the status of an account. Most worrisome was that no proposals were going out to potential new clients.

About a month after John ousted me from my office, I heard him coming down the hallway toward my new digs. *Every single morning*, I thought. The guy just wouldn't let up.

"Good morning, Rose."

Hearing him say my name startled me. He'd never said it before, so I looked up. When I did, he was standing in the doorway giving me the finger. I couldn't help it: I burst out laughing. He finally got me.

The next day, I didn't get a "Good morning" when he came into work.

"What's up, loser?" he said.

"*You're* the loser," I replied.

"Well, you're stupid."

"Not as stupid as you."

He's kind of funny, I thought.

By the summer of 1994, it wasn't just our little group at PR/NY that wanted to know what John was up to. The press was also beginning to wonder. A year had passed since he left the DA's office, and as far as they knew, he wasn't up to much. The media looked for drama: Was he striking out on his own, or headed for a breakdown? *People* magazine pounced on the theme with the sensational cover line: "Is he a man with a plan, or a dreamboat adrift?"

I grabbed the magazine, which I had seen on the newsstand on my way into work, and busted it out in our morning sparring session.

"Morning, dreamboat," I said when he walked into the office.

"Why don't you take that fright wig off? It's not Halloween," he retorted.

"Sorry we can't all be as handsome as you."

"Shut up, Rosie."

No one called me Rosie except my family. But somehow, I didn't mind John saying it; he was already starting to feel like the older brother I never had.

Our jokes had become a routine, a ritual we both enjoyed, like coffee from the cart or starting with Page Six when reading the papers. John could take it as well as he could give it, which was totally unexpected. And his jokes never felt personal. In fact, they were corny. I loved that our banter had stemmed from John standing up to me after I iced him out. He was as straightforward as I was and had no problem calling people out when necessary. His giving me the finger was just the first of many times I would see him challenge someone.

We were direct with everything, not just humor. When John first came into PR/NY after his mother, who by all accounts had been his emotional rock, passed away in May of that year, I didn't know what to say. I wondered if I should say anything at all. It's hard to know how to respond to the tragedy of an office mate. But he looked so somber, I couldn't pretend nothing had happened.

"Hi," I said.

"Hi," John replied.

"Sorry about your mom."

"Thank you, Rosie," he said, then gave me a hug, which I wasn't expecting.

"They say you don't really become an adult until both your parents are gone," he told me later.

John always seemed like an adult to me. We often talked about current events, and I'd ask what he thought had really happened behind the biggest story of the day. I liked his even take on the world and his way of putting any story into a balanced perspective. When President Richard Nixon died, I rolled my eyes while telling him that Nixon was my dad's man (Reagan was his other).

"Nixon was a brilliant man," John said.

I was shocked he didn't jump on the bandwagon and shit all over the disgraced president. Intelligent people see both sides of an issue, and John saw value in even the most flawed people, accepting that everyone makes mistakes.

It wasn't long after the "dreamboat adrift" cover line that Michael called me into his office again. I racked my brain for mistakes I'd made. There hadn't been much work to mess up; maybe that was the problem. When I got inside, Will was also in Michael's office, perched on a windowsill.

"Sit down," Michael said from behind his desk.

Oh, Jesus, I'm getting fired.

"We're selling PR/NY. Will's going to find something else,

and I'm—" Michael broke off for a second. "I'm going into business with John."

I knew it. I fucking knew it. Michael was jumping ship.

"Can't you take me with you?"

"It's not a PR thing, Rose. And everything is still up in the air. But don't worry. I've found you a new job."

"I don't want a new job. I want to stay here."

Michael had made me feel as though I was indispensable. He even said in one of my reviews, "You are the prize of my pen." I couldn't understand why he wouldn't want to take me with him.

"There is no 'here' anymore," he said. "I sold the business to another PR firm; all the accounts and you are part of the deal. You're going to work for them."

"What if I don't like it there?"

"Give the new firm a chance. Just go meet them." He handed me a slip of paper with a midtown address, and I arranged to be interviewed that afternoon. But as I made my way uptown to my potential new employer's office, I was furious at Michael for springing this on me at the last minute and still not telling me the whole truth. What was his business with John, and why couldn't he take me with him? In the elevator on my way up to the impromptu interview, I tried to tell myself that perhaps this was for the best. My new job might be even cooler than PR/NY. I had to keep an open mind.

But as soon as the doors opened, I knew there was nothing cool about the place. The reception area was set up like a tiki bar, with wood paneling and colored Christmas lights, in a sad attempt at being "fun" and "hip." I was going from a chic minimalist office to a Las Vegas lounge.

The receptionist sent me in to meet one of the executives, who had a typically drab office with slivers of window that looked out on the misery of midtown workers scrambling to grab lunch and get back to the office with enough time to actually eat it. When the woman stood up and extended her hand, a pungent, stale aroma wafted my way—she smelled like booze.

"Michael told me you're great with clients and really good at booking media."

Yeah, I thought, *a prize he was looking to give away.*

"I need you to write a press release so I can see your work," she said, slurring her words.

"Right now?" I asked. I was pretty nervous. I already knew I didn't want to work for this lady, but I needed a job. Without saying another word, she got up from her desk and wobbled away to make room for me to use her computer. I sat down in her chair and waited in silence for a few awkward moments. Had she passed out behind me?

"Well, what's it about?" I asked.

"What?" she said.

"The press release you want me to write."

"Oh, right . . . God is announcing the end of the world, and you have to write a press release."

She had to be kidding.

"Who is your client?" I asked.

"God."

I stared at the screen with my wrists resting on the keyboard, fingers poised to type, having no idea what to write. *There is no way I'm doing this,* I thought as I stared at the blinking cursor. I got up and looked right at her. "Well, if God is your client, then you don't need me, or a press release," I said, grabbing my purse and running out of her office.

I ran through the tiki-lounge waiting area to the elevators and repeatedly pressed the down button, hoping she wouldn't follow me. Nobody was in the elevator, and when the doors closed, I leaned against the wall and began sobbing. I was hysterical. Everything good about my life was slipping away. The job I had been lucky to get and worked so hard to keep was over. I wouldn't be hanging with people like Michael and John, or even Liz and Tricia, anymore. I would probably lose my apartment and have to move back in with Frank and his mom or, even worse, back home.

I cried all the way from midtown to 26th Street. Somewhere along the way, one of my contacts fell out of my eye, so by the time I got back to PR/NY, I was puffy, crying, and half-blind. I went straight into my office and slammed the door shut.

Moments later, Michael banged on the door and said, "Rose, come on, open up." But I wouldn't. I yelled through the door, "Forget it. I can't believe you're ditching me like this."

From the other side of the door, I heard John ask, "What's going on?" Then there was a low murmur as John and Michael talked about me. I heard one pair of footsteps retreating and gathered that John had returned to his office—which I still thought to be *my* office.

"Rosie, calm down."

It was John.

"I think we might be able to figure something out," he said. I worried he was going to give me a pity talk, but I opened the door anyway. Instead, he sat on the edge of my desk and looked me straight in the eyes. "Why don't you work for me?"

31

The fact that I really didn't want to leave moved John. I would come to understand that he prized loyalty above all. Plus, he liked my sense of humor; I made him laugh, and he wanted me to stick around. . . . Doing what, I had no idea.

"What will you do?" I asked.

John laughed. "I'm starting a magazine."

CHAPTER

2

"Random Ventures, please hold. Random Ventures, please hold."

Although I had pictured myself staying at PR/NY for much longer, promoting new brands and partying with Liz and Tricia, the company had been dissolved. Will jumped to another firm and brought his clients with him. Liz landed a job at a marketing company that did product tours in malls and would later come back to work with John, and Tricia went to work for Michael's girlfriend, Victoria Hagan, an interior designer.

Only three of us—Michael, John, and I—were left in the old offices, but the new business, Random Ventures, was much livelier than PR/NY had been, starting with the phone lines. Before John's arrival, the office was a quieter and slower-paced environment. Now it seemed frenetic, and the phones were ringing off the hook. My new job description included the role of receptionist. I felt like a switchboard operator, juggling lines and jotting down messages—all of them "urgent," at least according to the voices on the other end. The phones began ringing before I opened the door in the morning and kept on ringing long after I'd left.

Just answering the phones would have been fine. But I was more than overwhelmed spending all day answering questions—or, rather, avoiding them, since Michael and John's new enterprise was still a secret. Random Ventures started out as an idea to sell custom-made kayaks. Once John and Michael realized they couldn't mass-produce the handcrafted boats, they scrapped the plan and decided to start a magazine. When I joined Random Ventures, it was nothing more than the two of them looking for a publisher.

At that point, I didn't know what John and Michael were telling people about the company or whom they were telling it to, but they told me they wanted to keep word of their affairs quiet while they looked for a backer. Until there was a definitive plan, they hoped to keep their venture out of the news.

I soon found out, however, that nothing about John's life stayed quiet for long. As he gave his new office number out to friends and contacts, word of his whereabouts spread and the phones started going crazy. People weren't calling for Random Ventures; they were calling for John—even if they didn't know what he was doing.

Who knew it was possible to have that many friends? They wanted to meet for drinks, make dinner plans, or ask a small favor ("Please . . . just have him call me back. . . ."). Mountains of mail also poured into the chaotic new office, mostly letters from charities begging John to lend his famous name to this or that cause, each worthier than the last.

My nerves were frayed because I now had a million opportunities every day to say something stupid to the wrong person or piss off someone important. The less I said, the better, so I quickly devised a script for myself that was essentially "I'll see if he's in." And I stuck to it.

I didn't want to do anything to screw up their plan to start a magazine that blended the opposing worlds of politics and pop culture. The timing was right for their concept: politics was moving in a younger and decidedly more mainstream direction. A couple of years earlier, in June 1992, a young and charismatic presidential candidate from Arkansas named Bill Clinton had played his sax on *The Arsenio Hall Show* during his campaign. President Clinton (who later appeared on MTV, where he was asked whether he wore boxers or briefs, to which he answered, "usually briefs") was rewarded when election polls the year of his win showed a 20 percent increase in youth turnout over the prior presidential election, reversing a twenty-year decline of young voters.

Reaching out to young people through late-night shows was only part of the effort to change the long-standing conception of politics as uncool. Rock the Vote, a group that used music, celebrity, and pop culture to get young people interested in the political process and voting, was heating up with PSAs from artists like R.E.M., En Vogue, and Eddie Vedder, as well as TV specials featuring such A-listers as Madonna, Tom Cruise, and Chris Rock. I couldn't imagine anyone more suited to merge the two worlds of pop culture and politics than John, since he exemplified both.

While I didn't have an actual title at Random Ventures, it was clear from day one that my job was strictly administrative, assisting both John and Michael. In the beginning, that meant typing and mailing letter after letter to media companies and private investors that John and Michael viewed as potential backers. Getting a response was never a problem, since everyone wanted a meeting with John. Unfortunately, it soon became clear that an eager reply didn't necessarily indicate an intention to finance the political magazine. But John and Michael kept feeding me names from their Rolodexes, and I kept typing them into cover letters.

Had that been all it demanded, my new job would have been a cakewalk. But nothing with John was ever simple. His personal and public lives mixed in the most unique manner, and every detail was nuanced in a way that my upbringing hadn't prepared me for. What did I know about serving on the benefit committee of the Whitney Museum or attending the celebration of the newly restored Grand Central Terminal? Growing up, my idea of culture was the *Daily News*.

At first, I was at a total loss to understand his circumstances, and like many people who didn't know John well, I initially misinterpreted some of his behaviors as insensitive or spacey, when in fact they were coping mechanisms for his insane life. Take the fifteen-minute rule, for example. Whether attending a movie screening or meeting a friend for lunch, John was always right on time—which is to say, exactly fifteen minutes late. As his new assistant, I fielded more than a few panicked calls from people fearing they'd gotten the location wrong or, worse, were being stood up. But it didn't take long to figure out that John's tardiness was intentional—he was late because he couldn't risk standing on a street corner or at a restaurant bar if his appointment was running behind schedule. He'd be a sitting duck for anyone wanting an autograph or hoping to tell him a story about his mother or father. Hence the fifteen-minute rule. It even applied to one of his favorite pastimes, attending Knicks games, where he'd ease into his courtside seat long after the thousands of fans had already filed into Madison Square Garden.

Unfortunately, I had to figure that stuff out for myself. As foreign and enigmatic as John's life was to me, it was normal to him. He didn't deconstruct the details of his day; he acted on instinct, and I had to learn to do the same.

When I started working for him, I was unsure how to approach some of the minor details. For example, the first couple of times I booked his plane tickets, I wasn't sure how to refer to Kennedy Airport. I mean, should I say "JFK" or "Kennedy" or "the airport named after your father"? It was awkward. He finally said to me, "I don't mind going out of Kennedy," and that's the term I used from then on.

Reserving a hotel room for him for the first time was particularly confusing. I decided that using his name was out of the question, because it would cause havoc if people knew he was coming. Without asking him how he would like me to handle his travel arrangements—I hated to bother him with minutiae—I decided to reserve the room under my name. After I'd booked two or three trips like this, John approached me.

"Hey, Rosie, when you book my hotel room, it's okay to put it under my name."

"Oh, okay. I wasn't sure you wanted that, but I will from now on. Was there a problem?"

"Well," he said, his face breaking into a shit-eating grin, "I don't get the fruit basket, the upgrade, or the champagne when it's under your name. It sucks to travel as you, Rosie."

It also sucked to deal with all the crazies who loved John. Every celebrity has a contingent of fanatical admirers. But the depth of feeling that John evoked in many, many people—celebrities included—was over the top. Yet while there were plenty of magazine stories about him, alongside the obligatory picture of him flinging a Frisbee or dashing into a cab, for the most part John kept his private life private. The gap between people's intense interest and the little they actually knew about him allowed them to fill in details of their own choosing. They could easily superimpose their fantasies onto the blank slate of his public persona.

John was the perfect storm for those with obsessive tendencies: good-looking, famous, single, and part of a family with more conspiracy theories than cousins. What amazed me was that while many of his fans clearly didn't have a firm grasp on reality, they were extremely resourceful, always finding a way to track down his address or phone or fax number. Once, I watched our fax machine spit out seventeen pages of a completely unintelligible rant in small, serial-killer-like handwriting. Some would call, often starting out perfectly normal before rapidly descending into something along the lines of "I am the child of Marilyn Monroe." I became adept at feigning confusion and insisting the caller had the wrong number, confident that they wouldn't call back.

Although mostly freaks wrote to John, I think he got more letters than Santa Claus. At first, I'd just collect them and leave them in a carton on his desk. But one afternoon, I peeked into his office to see if he wanted something from the deli and found him opening an envelope with his engraved letter opener, a considerable stack untouched before him. Realizing how much time his mail consumed, I took on the task myself, for which John was wordlessly thankful.

I had to sift through mountains of Valentines and Christmas cards, photos and requests for autographs, packages and paranoid delusions, before arriving at his charity invitations, bills, and business correspondence. Imagining dark and lonely apartments where the writers furiously scribbled their mad thoughts, I felt sad for these people.

Early on, one particularly insane-looking missive landed on my desk. The address was written in tiny, precise capital letters on a nondescript white business envelope. The letter rambled on about homosexuality and other topics that didn't make a whole lot of sense. And the stationery felt sticky to the touch. I gagged and pushed the letter aside.

Later that day, John saw the empty envelope on my desk and smiled. "Ah, Robert," he said.

"Do you know him?"

"Sort of."

Hearing that he knew the guy, I was relieved I hadn't made fun of the crazy letter. Maybe he had an eccentric friend in a mental institution. Who knows?

"He's been writing to me since I was at Brown," John said. "He's nothing if not resourceful."

"Phew. I thought you were going to say he was your long-lost friend."

John looked at the letter for a beat before turning back to me.

"No," he said. "But if you're nice, I'll fix you up with him."

It wasn't just weirdos who reached out to John. Known for his sense of obligation to give back, he received many solicitations to lend his name to charitable causes. He couldn't respond to all or even most of the requests. But reading a particularly confident and upbeat letter (along with the cutest photo ever) from a ten-year-old boy about how much he loved his five-year-old brother, who had Down syndrome, I felt I had to do something for this kid. He was collecting business cards from famous people to raise money for his brother's school. "You would love my brother, too, if you ever met him," he wrote. After looking at that photo for what seemed like forever, I went into John's office and said, "You know I never ask, but I can't put this request down." After reviewing it, John said to leave it with him and he'd "figure something out." Not only did John send a business card and buy an ad in the program but he also wrote a personal letter to each of the brothers.

John was generous, but he wasn't nuts. He wasn't about to invite his unhinged admirers in for a cup of coffee. Still, that didn't stop many of them from showing up in person at the office, often traveling great distances to get there. As a result, I was concerned about John's security. He didn't seem to worry too much about his personal safety, but it was always in the back of my mind.

It didn't take a degree in psychology to distinguish the real threats from the annoying hangers-on—and it didn't take long to identify the wackos. They wore hats decorated with flowers or carried journals fat with clippings. More often than not they were in the process of saving the world and absolutely had to speak with John. They were his long-lost brother, his best friend, even the mother of his children.

One woman, who regularly sent index cards with food stamp covers attached to them, insisted he was the deadbeat dad of her kids and wanted to know where her child support was. "I will see you in court, John Kennedy," she wrote on the backs of the cards, which arrived at the office at least three or four times a week.

My job was to shield John from the onslaught of freaks, as we came to call them, so I didn't bother him with these incidents, even though some made for pretty funny stories. Like the lady who brought a suitcase to the midtown offices we later moved into and unpacked it in the middle of the reception area, or the time the receptionist, Aramenta, called to tell me that John's sister was at the front desk. I knew that couldn't be right—Caroline of all people would never make an unscheduled visit to the office—but I still raced to reception.

When I approached the front desk, Aramenta pointed to a heavyset woman in a stained turquoise sweat suit. As I got closer, I saw she was missing a tooth and had no laces in her sneakers. Aramenta, an elderly lady from the South and everybody's surrogate grandmother, was sweet but not the best security buffer.

"That's not John's sister, Aramenta," I said.

"I didn't think so," she replied, shaking her head. Like everything else I did for John, my role as his gatekeeper was never officially defined. It just happened naturally. If a particularly ardent fan was in the lobby, I'd pop my head into John's office and tell him to make a few more phone calls before leaving for the day, or I'd call him at home to say he should maybe hit the gym or run an errand before coming into the office. I used that code, even though he knew what I was talking about, because

I didn't want him to feel like a freak himself. John downplayed his fame, and I was following his lead.

My job didn't come with a training manual, and relying on instinct occasionally steered me wrong. Once when John asked me to decline an invitation, I fibbed to the hostess that he couldn't attend her event because he was going out of town for the weekend. That's the excuse I always used when I wanted to get out of something—but then again, I wasn't constantly followed by paparazzi. A huge half-page photo of John in the gossip section of the tabloids the following Monday caught me in my white lie. Whoops.

Many eyes were constantly on him, scrutinizing his every move, whether out of outsized affection or bitter jealousy. So such mistakes made John look bad and me look like a fuckup. Since my actions directly reflected on him, I became more vigilant. There was no margin of error.

I wish I had been more attentive while typing up a note for John to Mort Kondracke, the veteran journalist and executive editor of the Capitol Hill newspaper *Roll Call*. I sent such letters out several times a day, so I didn't think twice about it, until a few days later when I saw it reprinted in the *New York Post*. I had misspelled Kondracke's name.

Oh no, this is bad, I thought. Within minutes of the paper's arrival, John called me into his office. My hands were shaking and my heart was pounding when I heard John's voice tightly articulating my name. Stepping into his office, I realized it was worse than I'd feared. John was behind his desk, white-knuckling the paper. He was so mad that I tried a preemptive self-effacing remark to avoid getting chewed out.

"I'm so humiliated," I said.

He wasn't having any of it. "How do you think *I* feel? Like people don't think I'm dumb enough already."

I swore to him and to myself it would be the last time I was so careless.

But being a decent assistant isn't just about making your boss look good. I had to understand John's motivations and aspirations so that I could act on his behalf without embarrassing either of us. As with any relationship, figuring him out took time—and my screwups sometimes offered the best insight into the real John.

When John asked me to make a lunch reservation for two at La Grenouille, the legendary French eatery, I made the rare mistake of completely forgetting to call. He was planning to ask Marie-Josée Kravis, the glamorous economist wife of the billionaire financier Henry Kravis, to join him on the board of the Robin Hood Foundation, a charitable organization that fights poverty in New York City. John knew the elegant philanthropist would feel at home at the upscale restaurant. However, when they entered the dining room, the maitre d' had no reservation listed for John Kennedy.

John called the office from a pay phone (this was before cell phones) and lit into me.

"They don't have my name down. There's no reservation," he yelled. "What am I supposed to do, take her to Hamburger Harry's?"

I knew I'd messed up, but John's anger surprised me. He was always so laid-back. Had I misread him? Was he really an entitled asshole? I don't know if I was caught off guard or simply scared by his fury, but either way, I lied to him.

"I-I don't know what happened," I stammered. "I made the

reservation. Even if they don't have your name, won't they just seat you anyway?"

I mean, what restaurant couldn't find space for John Fucking Kennedy Jr.? Most places would bring a carpenter in to build a table just to have him sit in their restaurant.

"It doesn't matter. You don't just waltz into La Grenouille without a reservation," he said.

As soon as John slammed the phone down, I called the restaurant in tears and explained to some random French guy that I had forgotten to make the reservation, and then I pleaded with him to seat my boss.

"It eez no problem," he said when I finally took a breath. "They are already seated."

When John returned from lunch, I was petrified. I'd spent the past few hours organizing files to the point of hysteria. But he just flopped down in a chair, giving me his best puppy-dog eyes, which, as you can imagine, were pretty good, and said, "I'm sorry, Rosie. I shouldn't have taken it out on you. I was just embarrassed in front of Mrs. Kravis. I didn't want her to think I'm an arrogant prick who expects special treatment whenever he walks in the door. It's just disrespectful, you know?"

I appreciated John explaining why he was upset, but I didn't quite follow why he was apologizing.

"They cleared the whole thing up at the restaurant," he said.

"They cleared *what* up?" I asked nervously.

"The maitre d' said there was a mix-up because a new person was managing the reservations. He brought the book over and showed me that my name was put in for next week."

I didn't contradict the maitre d's story, though I was beyond grateful to him for covering my ass. I understood why John had been so angry. Unlike some celebrities, he didn't need to feed his ego by aggrandizing his image. He didn't throw his weight around to validate his existence; he didn't have to. There was not one person alive who was more famous than John F. Kennedy Jr. If the hottest movie star in the world was someplace and John showed up, the star would immediately turn into wallpaper. John worked to put people at ease—making reservations, writing thank-you notes, always following the proper protocol. He wanted to do things the right way, and so did I.

As soon as John left my office, I picked up the phone to find out the name of the coolest maitre d' in the world and send him the biggest bouquet of flowers I could afford. I was learning some manners of my own.

While I was busy learning manners from the master and fending off lunatics, John and Michael continued courting investors for the magazine. We could have carpeted the office floor with rejection letters—all *very* sincere in their regret, mind you, but rejections nonetheless. And so we were psyched when Hachette Filipacchi, the media company behind magazines such as *Elle* and *Car and Driver,* called to request a second meeting. After taking a call from a representative for David Pecker, the CEO, who had said they were interested in making a deal, John hung up with a combination of shock and sheer relief on his face.

"Wow. This might be it," he said.

The months of knocking on people's doors asking for money had taken a toll on John and Michael, two rich guys not used to going around town with their hats in their hands. All the skepticism and doubt brought on by rejection finally gave way to the possibility that their wacky magazine idea might actually change the world—and I would be part of it.

Unless . . . that's when a terrible thought and very real possibility dawned on me: *What if John and Michael don't take me with them to Hachette?* We'd never discussed the scope of my job, neither its duties nor its timeline. Maybe, once they got the magazine up and running, they planned on dumping me for someone with more experience or a better education. *What do they need* me *for? Why wouldn't they want someone more corporate, with some magazine experience?* I thought. The feeling crystallized when John and Michael said they were heading out for a celebratory drink and a strategy meeting.

On my way home, I walked through the small park near the office to clear my head, but even the perfect fall weather couldn't dispel my anxiety. By the time I opened the door to my apartment, I was in a total funk. I was convinced that I was back at square one; only now when I revised my résumé I'd have to put the title of assistant down as my current position instead of publicist. The white walls of my apartment had never felt smaller.

I had to talk to someone about my situation. The trouble was, not many people knew the identity of my current employer—except for Frank and my family, and Frank wasn't exactly a model career counselor. John hadn't asked me to, but I'd kept my role as his assistant secret from most people. I didn't want random friends asking me for autographed photos or out-of-the-way favors. More important, I was nervous about inadvertently leaking secret information to the wrong person.

So I erred on the paranoid side when it came to concealing my job, telling my friends that I was working for a new PR firm.

Once while talking to a guy I wanted to impress, I bragged that I worked for a magazine.

"Oh, which one?" he asked.

I panicked then and tried to dodge the question. "It's not one you've ever heard of," I replied dismissively.

"Try me."

I racked my brain. "*The Congressional Research Tribune.*"

"No, I've never heard of that," he said slowly. "Sounds technical."

"It's based out of DC" was all I could muster, and he instantly lost interest.

Okay, so I wasn't CIA material. All I knew was that if the press found out John was shopping a magazine, the leak wouldn't come from me. While I was learning all the nuances of being a discreet and dedicated assistant, I hadn't yet learned how to advocate for myself.

So I picked up the phone and called the one person I knew wouldn't ask a lot of annoying questions.

"Hey, Dad," I said into the receiver.

"Hi, honey," he said. "Hold on, I'll get your mother."

"No, Dad, wait. I want to talk to you."

"Oh, what's the matter?"

I dove right into my predicament. Talking a mile a minute, I explained that I wasn't sure John and Michael would be taking me with them and I didn't know how to ask.

"You're a smart girl with a lot of common sense and a good heart," my dad said. "They've already hired you, so what are you worried about?"

"Come on, Dad. These people have Ivy League degrees. They have money. They're completely hooked up. What the hell do they need from me?"

"Hey! What kind of stupid talk is that? Just because someone's got more money doesn't mean they're better than you. As a matter of fact, most people with money are the cheapest bastards in the world. Just because they've got cash doesn't mean they've got class. And it doesn't mean they owe you anything, *either*. What they've got is none of your business. What have I always told you and your sisters?"

"Act like you've been there before," I said, repeating the phrase I'd heard him say so many times.

"That's right," he said. "I don't care if you walk into a penthouse on Park Avenue, you just say, 'Nice place.' Don't make a production or tell them how much better it is than your place."

"I know, Dad, but this situation is not that simple."

"Yeah, it is. Listen, sweetheart, you already have everything. I bet these guys need you just as much as you need them."

At the office the next day, with my dad's pep talk fresh in my head, I waited a few hours after John came in before approaching him. I'd been trying to get up the nerve to talk to him all morning, turning my dad's words over and over in my mind as I continued the pep talk: *You're doing a good job. John likes you. He's comfortable around you. He doesn't have to censor himself or worry that you're untrustworthy. You're a Terenzio from the Bronx, which means you keep shit close to your vest. Most of all, John knows that if you have something to say, you'll say it to his face.*

I saw the light on his phone line go off and slowly walked

to his office, where John was squeezing a stress ball and reading the newspaper standing up.

"Can I ask you something?" I blurted out, startling him as I stood in the doorway.

"Sure, Rosie."

"Am I coming with you to Hachette?"

"Of course you are," he said. "You're a lifer, Rosie."

And just like that, everything was okay. Everything was more than okay; it was amazing. My dad was right. And now I was about to enter the ranks of New York's publishing elite alongside one of the country's most famous figures. I knew that lots of people—cooler, richer, and better educated than me— would kill to be in my position. I had no idea what I had done to deserve this. I just hoped it would last.

CHAPTER
3
___

The name *George* said it all. Paying homage to the country's first president, the title made clear the magazine's themes of patriotism, democratic engagement, and history. And its informality pushed the publication's pop side.

After the second meeting with Hachette, John and Michael's venture gained momentum. Over the next several months, they attended meetings and more meetings with the Hachette people and their lawyers, until the deal was formally announced in February 1995, on Washington's birthday (another of Michael's PR moves). I wasn't privy to the legal back-and-forth, but from my perspective, everything went smoothly. Everything except the naming of the magazine.

The name *George* was the brainchild of Daryl Hannah's brother-in-law Lou Adler, the record producer responsible for the Mamas and the Papas and Cheech and Chong. John and Michael loved it. Unfortunately, Hachette didn't feel the same way, and they were footing the bill. The company offered a bunch of horrible alternatives, including *Crisscross,* which, I guess, represented the juxtaposition of pop culture and politics. When John found out they wanted to change the title, he became incensed. But Michael talked him down, telling him everything would work out and that he had this one covered.

Sure enough, a few days later, an anonymous source leaked an item to Page Six that John Kennedy was starting a magazine— and it was called *George.* No one, not even the Hachette execs holding the purse strings, could take it back after that. Now the whole world was waiting to get their first copy of *George*—the title was a done deal.

For the first three months of *George*'s existence, the magazine was nothing more than John, the editor in chief; Michael, the publisher; and me, their assistant, locked in a conference room at Hachette's headquarters, a skyscraper with forty-eight stories of black glass and steel at Broadway and 51st Street and a far cry from the laid-back downtown vibe at PR/NY.

Located off a small, gray lobby on the 44th floor—and shared by several other Hachette magazines, including *Elle*— was our "office," a windowless conference room outfitted with three well-worn metal desks. So much for the glamorous image I had of New York publishing. We had three computers but only two phones, and no watercooler. I couldn't believe we were stuck in such a shabby hole—even if it was temporary. John, the anti-diva, joked, "This is the life," while I wondered if we wouldn't have been more comfortable setting up our new offices on a bench in Madison Square Park.

We didn't have time to brood over the claustrophobic setup, however; we had so much to do that we often worked right though lunch and dinner. (Best diet ever: I probably lost fifteen pounds during that time.) The conference room was flooded with résumés and portfolios as John and Michael set out to build an entire staff from executive editor to editorial assistant. The stakes were high as they searched for energetic and intelligent people who could fill in the knowledge gap left by their lack of editorial experience.

Everything was new and exciting—every person, position, and idea. But it was stressful, too. I had never worked at a magazine and couldn't fathom keeping up with the slew of well-read, socially adept editors or creative and chic designers with whom I imagined I'd be working. Before Michael and John had hired a single person, I decided they were all smarter, better-looking, and savvier than me.

Since I still hadn't told my friends about my new job, I wasn't able to unburden myself of these mounting insecurities. Not that it mattered much, since I spent all my time at work, where personal calls were out of the question. Sandwiched between Michael and John, I wasn't about to start whining into the phone, even to Frank. "It's so good to be this close," Michael said, laughing. "I feel like we're a little family." *Good?* I thought. *Speak for yourself.* I didn't breathe for the first three months.

Everyone in that building was dying to know what we were up to. From the producers at VH-1 to the security guy in the lobby, people were buzzing with curiosity about John and his mystery magazine. We were like a new toy.

Within those four cramped walls, I also got my first real taste of the lack of privacy that accompanied John wherever he went. At Random Ventures, we had been bombarded with phone calls and mail, but here, people were constantly coming in and out of the conference room throughout the day. They would find any and every reason to ask a question or be helpful, while we remained trapped behind our metal desks. Building maintenance guys came to replace lightbulbs that weren't burned out, and operations staff regularly checked our unchanging thermostat.

The female traffic was hilarious. Our neighbors, the *Elle* girls, turned John-spotting into an ongoing contest, keeping score on who saw him the most times in a day. Women in trendy outfits, barely able to stifle their giggles, made a well-worn path to our door.

That extra attention John was accustomed to quickly extended to Michael and me once people realized our association. All I had to do was walk into the lobby with John once, and from then on I got a super-friendly "Hello, and how was your weekend?" from the security guard. Employees I didn't recognize knew my name, and a couple of them even asked me to lunch. It reached the point where I was slightly paranoid about leaving the conference room, not sure what I would encounter on my way to grab a sandwich.

I also became somewhat spoiled—I wasn't about to let preferential treatment go to waste. I needed only to drop *my* name and someone from IT would race down to fix our computers. If I requested a fax machine, corporate asked, "Do you need a black or white one?" If someone from *Woman's Day* magazine asked for one, it could take months, if they got one at all.

Employees throughout the building came by to apply for openings at the new magazine. An art director at one of Hachette's titles asked me out on a date when he dropped off his portfolio. Although he was a little too old to be sporting a ponytail, I was psyched to go out with him—he was an insider and he was interested in me. He took me to Rodeo Bar, a Tex-Mex hangout with live music; we had a good time laughing over our common Italian heritage and gossiping about magazine publishing (my new profession!). During our second date, at a diner not too far from the office, he asked me about the position he'd applied for as *George*'s creative director. Surprised he didn't know that John had already filled it, I gave him the scoop. At the end of the meal, my portion of the bill—for a Greek salad and a Diet Coke—came to eight dollars, he informed me. *What the hell? He asked me out and now he wants me to pay?* I didn't have any cash, and the diner was cash-only. But he had a solution for that. "There's an ATM across the street. I'll wait here," he said.

My association with John was tricky—not everyone liked me just for me anymore. Ultimately, everyone wanted a connection to him, whether it was a job or just a sighting. Not long after we arrived at Hachette, a routine mention of John's personal life wound up in the paper. The untrue gossip item, which had him partying at a strip club, prompted an immediate visit from someone in the corporate communications department, who was overexcited about the opportunity to insinuate herself into the situation.

"How are we commenting on this?" she asked in a serious tone.

Michael just looked at her as if she were crazy—and dumb. "We aren't going to do anything," he said dryly.

In that instant, Michael set the PR strategy for *George*. It was about promoting a magazine, not a person. He was not about to hand that responsibility over to a corporate flack. She exited the conference room, clearly upset, and held a grudge against us that only strengthened the insularity of our group as we closed ranks within that big company.

Although the core idea behind *George* was still hazy to curious onlookers and the general public, for the three of us, the mission was crystal clear: John and Michael were determined to get people interested in politics. To the outside world, John might have appeared apolitical, a dilettante coasting along on his looks and money, a "dreamboat adrift." But in reality, John was ardently civic-minded. He wanted to bring disaffected young people into the democratic process by getting them hooked on the characters and behind-the-scenes stories of political life. According to him, those narratives were just as fascinating, horrifying, and inspiring as any gossip item or made-for-TV movie. Once people knew their congressman or mayor as well as they did the latest movie star, he reasoned, they would be more apt to care—and vote.

By the spring of 1995, *George* had moved out of the conference room and into its own dedicated space. It was worth the wait. John had the quintessential corner office, just like you see in the movies. Two walls of waist-to-ceiling windows offered sweeping views of the Hudson River to the west and Central Park to the north. It was perfect for John, who loved running or Rollerblading in the park and would often launch a kayak into the river after work. I thought he was nuts to get anywhere near the Hudson River. If a drop of that disgusting river water touched me, I'd have to shower in bleach.

George's logo—in huge yellow letters—now hung proudly

down the long corridor leading to the new offices and cubicles that were quickly filling up with staffers. I sat outside John's office and continued to be an assistant to both Michael and John, until it became clear that they each needed their own. I went with John, since Michael reasoned it was easier to find an assistant for him than for John.

I hadn't been wrong about the type of person the publishing world attracted. Some of the first editors to join the magazine were guys with Ivy League diplomas and pretty privileged backgrounds. There were a few women, and probably a few graduates from small liberal-arts colleges, but they were in the minority. Those guys would come into the office having read and watched everything—it was intimidating. Most *George* editors were ambitious, but some would stroll in at 10:30 a.m. and think nothing of taking two hours for lunch, even if it meant working late nights and weekends. From my desk in the hallway outside John's office, I had a front-row seat to the insular world of New York media, which sometimes seemed less like a profession and more like a popularity contest.

Cliques quickly formed, and there were two or three who perceived themselves as "serious journalists." They overdid the "we don't care what John says" thing. They took any opportunity to drive home the idea that they were at *George* to do the important stories and not to work for JFK Jr. In reality, everyone wanted to impress John. In that bizarre version of high school, he was the ultimate homecoming king.

They all competed for time with him. In fact, lunch became a real problem as the magazine evolved. If one editor had lunch with John alone, then another would come up to me—the paranoia and jealousy palpable—and say, "Why was *he* at lunch with John?" Always the peacekeeper, John made an effort to eat with each editor, so that all would feel important. It got so out of control that at one point he was going to lunch with each of them once a week (until I, the hall monitor, put my foot down).

In the three months leading up to the publication of the first issue, there was not a day off to be had. Everyone bitched and moaned about how late we were working—still, people didn't go home. We bonded over working at a magazine everyone was talking about. For the first time, those editors weren't just covering the news; they were making it. With all that newfound attention, actually getting the magazine out seemed secondary.

I was as guilty as the rest of the staff of getting swept up in the hype. I stayed late and came in on the weekends when it wasn't totally necessary. It wasn't like John's mail needed opening on a Sunday, but I didn't want to miss anything. Though I didn't know the difference between a managing and an executive editor, I was just as excited as anybody else about putting a new magazine on the racks. I loved the frantic highs and lows of the deadlines, the cynical banter between writers, and the debates about politics.

I loved being involved . . . until I realized I wasn't a member of the club. At first, I ignored hints from some of the staff, like the incredulous looks when I mentioned that I was a fan of the *New York Times* writer Frank Rich or that I had gone to college. I didn't see myself the way they saw me: as an unsophisticated assistant from the outer boroughs. John's secretary. A dumb girl with a Bronx accent. No one worth knowing.

I clearly didn't fit into their "George Plimpton at Elaine's" vision of magazine publishing, where men with Upper East Side addresses drank like tough guys and spent like heiresses while talking over the "important" stories. When they went out, it had to be to someplace where Hemingway took his last drink or Tom Wolfe first donned the white suit. And of course, at first I was not included. ("Well, if I were you, I certainly wouldn't go," a female editor who was part of their group said to me after I inquired about another editor's birthday-drinks outing. "He was *very* specific about who he invited.") That one particularly stung because the editor having the birthday was one I had a huge crush on—and he knew it.

Once, when most of the editorial staff was out of the office at a group lunch, John returned from a meeting to find me at my desk.

"Oh, you didn't have to wait for me to get back," he said. "You could have gone to lunch with everybody else."

"I wasn't invited," I said quickly.

"What? Why?"

"They never invite me."

I could tell John was annoyed. He didn't tolerate people being slighted. "Come on, we're going to lunch," he said.

He took me to the place where the rest of the staff was eating, and we sat three tables away, laughing and gossiping. I didn't need to look over at their table to know they got the message.

No lunch was going to change the fact that a few of the editors perceived me as a caricature of myself. They put on airs to hype what they perceived to be the mythic image of a magazine editor.

Their pretensions would have been funny if their assumptions about me didn't hurt so much. At any moment, someone could cut me down by reminding me where I came from. Especially if he felt threatened.

Once, an editor asked me to put a breakfast with him, John, and the head of PBS into John's calendar.

"Does he know about it?" I asked.

"Don't worry. It's fine," the editor said in a patronizing tone.

Keeping John's appointment book was tough. I had to be diligent, because people were always trying to sneak their personal agendas into John's calendar. He could barely even accomplish all his tasks for the magazine, let alone cater to everyone else's needs. Of course, when I ran the PBS breakfast by John, it wasn't okay with him.

I broke the bad news to the editor, perhaps with a little more enjoyment than I should have.

"Oh, that breakfast? I checked it with John, and he's not going," I said.

He gave me a snide look and said, "Do you even know what PBS is?"

I became more self-conscious, and because of that, I tried to hide my ignorance, not only of the magazine production process but also of current events. And frankly, there was a lot I didn't know. Books, politicians, artists—a whole world of culture opened up around me. But I refused to give those editors the satisfaction of letting on that I was out of my depth.

Although I didn't want the staff to think I was stupid, I absolutely didn't mind if they thought I was tough. I played the part of the Bronx badass, amping up my foul-mouthed persona with eye rolls and a fuckload of expletives (even though I never swore growing up: an F-bomb out of my mouth would have merited a swat to the head). I wanted them to be a little scared of me, but I also did it for John, who loved my Bronxy facade. When I strung together four or five curse words by way of an answer, he found the sassy street attitude charming.

John, in return, was my Henry Higgins. He was the one I asked about books and politicians I was unfamiliar with, and he never made me feel stupid. Not even once. He wasn't going to judge. (He himself got creamed in the press for failing the bar twice.) John was also a champion of trying to better oneself. "Rosie, you're savvy for asking the question," he'd tell me.

Everyone else on staff was like a satellite in orbit, moving in and out of my focus depending on his position in relation to John. I did make friends at the magazine, and many of those friendships still stand, but at the time I wondered whether people actually wanted to be my friend or just wanted to get close to John. *He* was the one to point that out—about members of his own staff: "You have to be careful of people who are vying for your friendship because of your proximity to me, Rosie."

That their motives were clear to John made the circumstances even more upsetting, because he didn't look for pettiness. So if it was obvious to him, it was obvious to everyone else, too—except for me. I didn't recognize the games people played because I didn't want to. My desire to be part of the group trumped my judgment, and I overlooked insincerity. Once John made me face the plain truth, I realized I needed to make a decision: Did I want to be popular, or do a good job? Choosing the latter, I became *a lot* more careful about what I said and to whom I said it. Of course, that pissed people off, but it was clear to John where my allegiance lay, and from that point forward he gave me more responsibility.

I gained access to information about the magazine—who

was going to be on the cover, or who was about to be fired—before the editors did. And in publishing, information is king. For those reasons, I was more relevant than an ordinary secretary, and yet I felt I could never live down my title.

The only person other than John who understood me was Matt Berman, who coincidentally had the same last name as Michael. We were an unlikely pair: the creative director with sophisticated taste in everything from film to furniture and the smartass assistant who thought of posters as art. But we shared a deep love of poking fun at people and often practiced our best imitations over dinner or drinks. As our friendship developed, some people at work could not believe he actually liked me as a person. "Everyone knows why you hang out with Rose," a coworker once said to him. "It's only because she's John's assistant and you want the inside info."

But I wasn't always on the inside. One day late in the summer of 1995, I was on the phone with Frank (he was partying too hard and needed a "come to Jesus" moment), when the conference room door burst open and everyone piled out laughing and talking loudly. When John gathered the staff in the conference room for editorial meetings, the office grew quiet, and my desk, where it was normally as easy to concentrate as in Grand Central Station, became a hushed Zen sanctuary. I used those infrequent and fleeting moments to tackle projects that required more thought than did booking a table for lunch or—shocker!—to make a private phone call.

"What's going on over there?" a groggy Frank asked.

"I gotta go," I said. "I'll see you tonight. Don't be late."

Now that the peace and quiet was over, I hung up the phone and stood to check out the scene: the editors were buzzing around John, which was totally normal, but they were all looking down at something in his hands that I couldn't see and saying over and over how great it was. The level of enthusiasm was highly unusual. And John led the charge. I had to find out what was going on.

As soon as the excitement died down, I popped into John's office.

"Jesus, what's going on? Did you hand out pictures of yourself to the whole staff?" I joked.

John looked up, smiling, with an expression on his face that I hadn't seen before. Happiness mixed with pride.

"Ha-ha, very funny," he said in a mock sarcastic tone. "I don't know if you know what it is that we do around here all day, but we're actually putting out a magazine. And here's our first copy."

As he waved the thick, glossy issue in the air, my heart sank. He and Michael had called everyone in to look at the first issue—except me. Staring at the cover girl, a bewigged Cindy Crawford dressed as George Washington, with exposed abs that would have made the first president blush, my throat tightened. I wanted to share in his excitement, and I *was* excited to see the first issue, which we had all worked so long and hard to put together, but the fact that he'd left me out of the grand unveiling hurt my feelings. I'd been at *George* since the very beginning—we were "a little family," according to Michael—and I thought they valued my efforts. The editorial staff might have been smarter, better educated, and more experienced, but no one cared as much as I did. For the past six months, I worked harder than I had at any other job (I hadn't had a day off for three weeks straight), but just like that, every insecurity I had was reinforced; I was just a dumb secretary again.

As I stood there trying to fight off tears, John's face clouded over with anger. "What's your problem?" he asked.

"I've been working my ass off and have had no life for about a year, and you can't even show me the magazine?" I started to cry.

"You know what?" he snapped, stuffing the magazine in a manila folder as if in punishment. "If this is the way you're going to behave, you can just go home."

I fled his office like a schoolgirl who had been admonished by the principal and returned to my desk. John closed his door, but I didn't go home. Instead I sat there—with red, puffy eyes, sniffles, and all. Nobody asked me what was wrong. Minding your business is the unwritten rule when dealing with those who have to cry without the privacy of an office, and I was a crier.

John stayed out of my way that afternoon. Whenever he left his office, he skirted my desk without making eye contact. Crying and drama, especially when he was the cause, irritated him and made him retreat into a cold, protective shell. It felt cruel, though. As warm and welcoming as John was, he could be equally distant and punishing. Like everyone else, I wanted something from him—I wanted him to understand why I was upset, and felt betrayed and fooled that he didn't.

When the clock neared quitting time, I collected my things and prepared to meet Frank for a much-needed drink. I shut down my computer and steeled myself to say good night to John, which I did every day before I left. I lightly knocked on the door, and then opened it. John was sitting at his desk, looking through the day's messages.

"Is it okay if I go? Do you need anything else?" I asked.

"It's fine. You can go," he said without looking up.

I almost threw up. *I ruined everything,* I thought. Why had I cried? My outburst was so unprofessional. I had no right to expect anything from him. He was my boss. All he owed me was a paycheck.

Nothing could cheer me up, not even Frank ordering a second round of our new favorite drink, dirty martinis. I was defeated, a feeling that stuck with me all night and into the next morning as I opened John's mail at my desk. John called me into his office almost as soon as he arrived.

That couldn't be good. He was going to fire me, I was sure of it. My throat was choked with a fresh round of tears, but I squared my shoulders and opened the door to find John hunched over his desk, looking up at me.

"Take a seat," he said. He looked serious, and I readied myself to hear a lecture about what's required in a professional workplace.

"I'm sorry, Rosie," he said.

The sincerity of his words was so plain that I thought I would start bawling again out of gratitude and relief.

"That was really rude and insensitive," he continued. "I should have showed the magazine to you first. I should have showed it to you before they saw it. I totally apologize."

John meant what he said, and the gentleness he showed in that moment overwhelmed me. I wasn't used to such generosity.

"Thank you" was the only reply I could muster.

He pulled up a chair and took out the magazine so he could show me the pages. The cover was stunning. Matt had come up with the concept after finding an Alberto Vargas illustration of a pinup girl in a tight Revolutionary War–style jacket and no pants. John had pulled a favor to get the edgy fashion photographer Herb Ritts, instead of a typical portrait photographer, to shoot the most sought-after supermodel in the country dressed as George Washington—an image that symbolized American success on steroids. It paid off; I had never seen a magazine cover like it and was sure no one else had, either.

"It's awesome. Congratulations," I said. Before I walked out of his office, I turned and added, "By the way, you aren't signing any of these. Because if you sign one, you'll have to sign thousands."

John just laughed and said, "You're right. New company policy."

When I returned to my desk, there was a message from Carolyn Bessette, the woman John had been dating for several months. I immediately called her back.

"Hi, honey, what's going on over there?" she asked. The two of us had quickly developed a friendly rapport in the time I had been working for John. We talked almost every day, first brief conversations when she called for John, then longer gossip sessions when she called for me.

"Did John apologize?" Carolyn asked.

"Yeah, he did. How did you know?"

"He came home last night a nervous wreck and told me the whole story," she said. "I said to him that I couldn't believe he showed all those other losers the magazine first and left you sitting outside like the redheaded stepchild. I told him, 'Oh no. You need to go in and apologize to her in the morning. That was really gross.'"

Carolyn came to my defense by making John feel like shit

about what he'd done, which was so typical of her. She always protected me, although at our initial meeting I never would have guessed that would be the case.

When she first walked into the offices of Random Ventures about a month after its formation, she was exactly the kind of girl I imagined would date someone like John—and she intimidated the hell out of me. Wearing a Calvin Klein pencil skirt, a white T-shirt, stiletto heels, and blue nail polish, she looked like a model, effortlessly perfect in an unstudied yet elegant outfit.

Carolyn and John had dated briefly in 1993 and reunited in 1994, a few months after his mom passed away. When John introduced us, I felt like I'd gained ten pounds and shrunk three inches. But after he left her in the reception area to deal with something in Michael's office, I could tell Carolyn was different from the typical gorgeous girls you see around Manhattan. Women who have attitude always stand in a pose, like they're trying to be sexy and intimidating, even if they're in line at the supermarket. Carolyn's easy posture said it all: standing with her legs crossed, she held her small, black patent-leather Prada purse behind her back with one hand, while absentmindedly twisting a lock of hair with the other. She wasn't trying too hard. In fact, she wasn't trying at all.

The phone kept ringing as Carolyn and I tried to make small talk. Finally she said, "Does it ring like this all the time?"

I nodded.

"You poor thing."

I smiled, pressing a button on the phone. "Random Ventures," I said as I answered another call.

"Hi, is this John Kennedy's office?" a woman asked.

"May I ask who's calling?" I said.

"Where are you located?" the caller asked.

"Is there something I can help you with?"

"Does he come into the office every day?"

The caller was trying to get way too much information. I wanted to end the conversation without being rude, and I had to think fast. It didn't help having Carolyn about two feet away. "John Kennedy?" I said. "Oh, I've never even met him. I *wish* he came here every day, miss. But this is an answering service. We just dispatch calls and take messages. So if you want to leave a message, I can take it down and get it to the right person."

"No, that's okay. Thanks," the woman said, and then hung up.

"Wow, you're good," Carolyn said.

John, having returned to the reception area, found us laughing.

"What are you two cackling about?" he asked.

We looked up at him like two kids caught in the act.

"Nothing," Carolyn said.

John and I didn't talk about his personal life when I first began working for him. He was a typical guy with no desire to hash out with me the intimate details or thoughts about his dates. However, I knew Carolyn was becoming an important part of his life because whenever she phoned the office, he always took the call. The only other person he did that with was his sister.

From the beginning of their relationship, it was obvious they were at ease around each other, the way friends are. Once we moved to Hachette in February 1995, Carolyn would come into the office and sit at John's desk, making phone calls as if it were her own. Or she would go directly to see Matt Berman, whom she loved, and hang out with him for a while before she even said hello to John. She didn't feel the need to run in to her boyfriend and announce herself. Carolyn wasn't John's shadow; she was his equal. He would ask her, a fashion insider who worked for Calvin Klein, about cover choices or get her advice on approaching designers and advertisers.

From my point of view, John was happier when Carolyn was around. And Carolyn, like any smart woman, had a way of making John pay attention to things he didn't necessarily want to even think about. She got him to differentiate between the people taking advantage of his generosity and those who needed a little extra attention from him. With those two circumstances alone, Carolyn made my life much easier.

CHAPTER
4

Carolyn always made me feel attractive and smart. And according to her, there was no better self-esteem booster than great fashion. "Nothing feels better than new clothes," she'd say. "That and vodka are your new best friends."

Carolyn had the best taste, so when she suggested a shopping trip—with her acting as my personal stylist—I was beyond excited. But I was also a little nervous. I pictured huge price tags and tiny sizes: way out of my league.

So when John said he needed me in the office around noon on the Saturday of our shopping expedition, I was relieved. But when I called Carolyn to relay the news, I couldn't talk her out of our plan.

"No problem," she said. "The stores open at ten o'clock. We have plenty of time. Just meet me," she said. "We'll shop for an hour, max. We need to get you a few good jackets and skirts."

When we arrived at Barneys, I was immediately over-whelmed by all the beautiful things. Carolyn knew exactly where to find outfits that worked for me, and she knew precisely what to pick out.

"Try this on, Rosie," she said, grinning, as she held up an eight-hundred-dollar Ann Demeulemeester leather skirt.

She had found the perfect piece for me—the gorgeous, very expensive version of me. I immediately launched into the kind of fantasies that amazing clothes induce: I could wear it with combat boots for a romantic date or with a blazer to a high-powered work meeting. But instead of grabbing the skirt out of her hands, I said, "I don't want to try it on."

Even though I was a size four from all the cigarettes I'd smoked and all the lunches I'd skipped, I was convinced there was no way I could wiggle into that slim leather skirt, and I didn't want to put myself through the embarrassment of having to try a bigger size. It wasn't just my size that bothered me; it was everything about my looks.

For as long as I could remember, I felt ugly. When I was a child, my aunt Rita (who wasn't actually my mom's sister but, rather, her best friend from the moment she moved in three houses down from ours) used to tell the same story about my birth at every holiday or family gathering: After first seeing me as a newborn in the hospital, Rita had such an expression of pity and disappointment on her face that the horrified nurse asked, "What's wrong?"—to which Rita replied, "She looks like her mother!"

She'd deliver the punch line to big laughs—every time. So the gag continued for years. I wanted to crawl under the table but instead laughed along with everyone else so as not to draw any more attention to the joke. (And my family always wondered why I never brought guys home for them to meet.)

My mom had her own riff on the same theme. Whenever someone said, "Marion, RoseMarie looks just like you," her response was always, "I know, the poor kid." Along with her looks, I also inherited her penchant for sarcasm. From the moment I became a teenager, I followed in my mom's footsteps, keeping my guard up with jokes at my own expense that masked any insecurities or yearnings.

It took me a long time—and some geographic distance from the Bronx—to realize that my mom was actually pretty. She had a great smile and a quick-witted sense of humor (she also had great boobs and great legs). But she lacked confidence in her femininity, and obscured her best features: chopping off her beautiful, thick, dark hair with the excuse that she didn't have time to waste worrying about it.

Unsurprisingly, self-deprecation came naturally to me, but Carolyn was the one person who wouldn't stand for it. Whenever I put myself down with a wisecrack about my appearance— such as, "I'm funnier than you because I look like *me,* and you look like *you*"—she reacted as though I had personally offended her. "Don't you dare say that," she would admonish. "You're beautiful and have the kind of body that boys love. You're so sexy, Rosie, and you don't even know it."

That tiny leather skirt from Barneys, Carolyn knew, would give me a boost of confidence.

"Try it on!" she said.

The next thing I knew, I was on my way to the cash register with the skirt, which fit like a glove, and—at Carolyn's insistence—"a shirt that goes with the skirt but doesn't match, a jacket that kind of matches, and pants to go with the jacket."

Headed to the cashier with thousands of dollars' worth of merchandise, I woke up from the whirlwind of playing dress-up and realized I couldn't afford any of it. "You know what, Carolyn? I'm just going to take the shirt," I said, trying not to be obvious while picking the least expensive thing in the pile. "I don't need the rest of it."

"No," she said firmly, and handed her credit card to the salesperson. "We're going to take all of it."

Carolyn understood how lucky she was to be able to afford beautiful clothes, and she wanted to share the wealth with those she cared about. I loved the clothes and her generosity, even if I was uncomfortable with the extravagance of the gesture.

After she reluctantly agreed to put back two of the items, I looked at my watch and quickly found something much worse to be upset about than the pile of money she had just spent on me. It was nearly one o'clock. I was an hour late for work! That was something I had nightmares about, not something I did in real life.

Carolyn tried to calm me down as I spiraled into total panic.

"I'll call John later and tell him we went shopping," she said. "It'll be fine."

Fine? In my world, being late to work was about as fine as showing up naked. I decided not to waste time finding a working pay phone to call and say I'd be late. What would my excuse be, anyway? *Sorry I couldn't show up for work on time, John. I was busy. Your girlfriend was just buying me a new wardrobe.* Instead, I dove into a cab and proceeded to lose my mind.

As I walked past reception, a sweaty mess, John was standing in the hallway talking to an editor.

"Well, look who decided to grace us with her presence," he said.

"I'm sorry."

"Apparently not sorry enough to show up on time."

John was pissed at me all day. But for once, I didn't beat myself up. I'd had the best time with Carolyn—and not just because she bought me the most beautiful clothes I'd ever seen. The shopping trip, which marked Carolyn's officially becoming my style fairy godmother, was her way of contributing to my success.

Confident in my abilities from the get-go, she wanted me to be respected in the role of John's assistant. She understood that if I wanted to get respect, I had to look the part. People *do* judge a book by its cover, especially in an industry as superficial as the media. She wanted others to see in me what she saw.

Within the first year of our friendship, I went through a complete style transformation under Carolyn's enthusiastic guidance. She didn't introduce me to fashion, but previously I had conflated trend with style (probably due to the influence of my sister Andrea, who was named "best dressed" in high school, having spent her entire paycheck from her cashier's job at Gristedes buying the latest looks from Bloomingdale's). Carolyn proved that I didn't have to look obvious to be sexy and that I could wear classic styles but make them my own.

As Carolyn had expected, my new clothes changed how people perceived me. Even John took note. A week after the shopping spree that landed me on his shit list, I got up the courage to wear one of my new outfits to the office.

"Whoa, Rosie," he said. "You look nice. Where are you going all dressed up? It certainly can't be for work."

"I have a job interview," I said, joking.

Carolyn's makeover didn't stop at clothes. Standing back and looking at my dark, curly Italian hair, she pronounced that I should get highlights, insisting I go to the top guy in the business. *Her* guy.

"You have such light skin, highlights would be so pretty and would brighten up your face," she said. "Next time I go to Brad Johns, you'll come with me."

Brad Johns was *the* colorist. All the best blondes in the city went to him. He was famous for inventing that rock-and-roll blond hair with chunky strips of lighter and darker colors. So I found myself entering Brad's Fifth Avenue salon, a bright, bustling space where everyone except me was blond. A muscular guy with, yes, blond hair flowing down to his shoulders ran up to greet Carolyn with a kiss on both cheeks. It was Brad.

"Hi, honey," he said. "What's new?"

"This is Rosie, John's assistant. And Rosie is the *best,*" she said, pushing me in front of him. "She's here to get her hair done."

Brad didn't really *do* hair anymore—he usually instructed his employees on how to do it. But that day, he sat me down to do my hair. He explained how he was going to soften my base color from a dark brown to a honey brown and add highlights in gold, wheat, and lemon.

Carolyn, sensing my unease (mostly from my staring in the mirror at my mass of black curls among this sea of blond), put her hand on my shoulder and said, "Don't be scared. You'll look gorgeous."

Through the next several hours of washing, dyeing, streaking, and blow-drying, about a dozen staff people approached to ask if they could get me coffee, tea, sandwiches, wine, champagne—whatever I wanted. I felt as if I were in a movie, as an emaciated girl with a white-blond bob brought me a flute of champagne, after a little gay man with an ash-blond crew cut had cleared away my cappuccino cup. I also felt like a fraud. Worried they'd find me out if I didn't come clean, I wanted to tell them: *I am not one of these people. You don't have to pull out all the stops for me.*

Brad proved Carolyn right: my hair looked gorgeous. I'd never had it professionally straightened and couldn't believe how soft and sexy it felt on my shoulders. And the color completely changed my face. My dark inheritance receded into the past. I loved it.

No one loved my new look more than Frank—certainly not a particular *George* editor, who snickered and whispered behind my back that I was copying Carolyn. (Well, if Carolyn Bessette wanted to buy me a wardrobe or take me to her colorist, what did they expect me to do, turn her down?) When we went out with friends, Frank showed me off: "Look at her fabulous coat!" Occasionally, he took it too far—like when we visited his mother around my birthday, and she apologized that she didn't have a gift for me: "I bought you a blouse from Macy's, but Frank said you'd never wear anything from Macy's." Mortified that his mom would think I had become a terrible person, I yelled, "Frank, how dare you!" and set the record straight.

Frank's passion for glamour caused him to intermittently put on airs, but I knew it made him perfect for the job of PR director at Brad's salon. As soon as I heard Brad was looking to fill the position, I began scheming. Frank was essentially incapable of finding employment for himself. So not only was I constantly trying to secure jobs for him but I also wanted to bring him along for the ride. I wanted Frank to experience the same kinds of perks that my job offered.

Carolyn seconded the idea. She knew that Frank was gorgeous—six foot two, with George Clooney salt-and-pepper hair—sweet, funny, and charismatic. The life of the party, he could talk to anyone and got along with everyone. The female beauty editors at women's magazines, whom Brad needed to woo, would adore Frank after he doted on them and made them feel special.

Carolyn and I concocted a plan: drinks at El Teddy's, a Mexican joint and Tribeca institution, topped with a giant replica of the Statue of Liberty's crown, that had been serving killer margaritas for more than twenty years.

Frank and Brad hit it off right away, which was no surprise. If you were a gay guy sitting across from Frank, you were into Frank. A few margaritas later, Brad offered him the job of PR director, a plum position that paid well and promised the start of a new life.

But the biggest coup came two days later, when Page Six printed an item about Brad and Carolyn dining at El Teddy's with "two fashionistas." At first I wondered whom they were talking about, then realized: *Frank and I are the fashionistas!* Having grown up reading the *New York Post*, I couldn't believe I was in it—and in the same sentence as the word *fashion*. It was amazing. Frank called me at work every day for the entire week after the item appeared and yelled into the phone, "I'm a fashionista!"

My friendship with Carolyn was about more than shopping sprees and trips to the hair salon. She and I shared a bond in that we both lived in John's unique world—although, obviously, in very different ways. I was often the only person who could relate to what she was going through. "I know this is kind of sad, but there's no one else I can talk to," she said one night, having fled to my studio after an argument with John. I could certainly relate; the burden of being close to someone so famous meant you had to watch everything that came out of your mouth. But Carolyn recognized that her visit put me in an awkward position as his assistant. "Don't tell him I came here," she said. "I don't want him to feel uncomfortable that I talked to you."

First thing in the morning, I walked into John's office and told him where Carolyn had been the night before.

"Look, you can get mad about this and have a huge fight with her, but she'll think I'm a tattletale trying to cause trouble," I said to John. "If you cause a rift between us, it's going to make your life harder and mine a living hell."

I told John the truth because, I reasoned, if Carolyn had decided to tell him herself, he might have wondered what else I wasn't telling him, and someone in my position couldn't afford that. I didn't want to get in the middle, but I was trying to be honest with both of them and also protect myself.

After talking to John, I returned to my desk and called Carolyn.

"Hey, sweetie, just in case John brings it up, I told him you came over last night to hang out."

"Okay. What did he say?"

"Nothing."

"He probably would have dragged it out of you somehow."

We both knew that wasn't true, but it signaled that she understood the boundaries: no matter how much I cared about her, my allegiance was to John. Ultimately, she knew that because John could trust me completely, so could she.

More than anyone else, Carolyn saw how fiercely loyal I was and the extent of my work for John, and because of it, she loved me and was one of my biggest advocates. We were a pretty good team, too. Sometimes she would call me in the morning before John had made it into the office to give me a heads-up on the state of his mood and the reasons for it. If he had an issue with me—such as, I was spending too much time answering the phones and not concentrating on drafting an important letter—she let me know. I was already adept at reading John, but Carolyn made me seem like a genius.

It took two hyperorganized women to manage John. Everything was chaos with him. The first time he and I traveled together, the problems began before we even stepped inside the airport. He asked me if I had his ticket, which of course I did, but I decided to give him shit.

"No," I said, deadpan.

"What? Are you kidding me, Rosie?" he asked, sounding panicked.

"I'm joking."

"Oh, by the way," he said, "I forgot my wallet."

Great.

Matt Berman, John, and I were headed to Nashville to shoot and interview Garth Brooks for the *George* cover. John couldn't miss the flight. As this occurred pre–September 11, the chance of American Airlines personnel denying him a boarding pass because he didn't have his ID was slim; however, John was traveling to Europe directly from Nashville, and he definitely needed his wallet and passport to go abroad.

I told John and Matt to check in while I ran to a pay phone and called FedEx. Sure enough, they had same-day service to Nashville, so with FedEx holding on one phone, I called Carolyn on the adjacent pay phone to make arrangements for FedEx to pick up John's wallet and passport.

She sighed in mock exasperation—moments like this with John were routine—and joked, "Better you than me."

While Carolyn gathered the necessary documents and John's wallet, and I sorted out the final details, John came over and pointed at his watch. "Rosie, what are you doing on the phone? We're going to miss the plane."

"I'm getting a psychic reading from Dionne Warwick. What do you think I'm doing?"

On the plane, he didn't even ask if I'd resolved the issue. Once he told me about his forgotten wallet, I sensed his relief. It wasn't his problem anymore; it was mine. He knew I'd take care of it. I always did.

John looked out for me, too. He wanted to come to my rescue if someone treated me badly, and he tried to do just that after my run-in with Barbra Streisand's assistant. The iconic singer-actress had posed as Betsy Ross for the cover of *George,* and although the deadline was fast approaching, the photographer still hadn't delivered the images. John asked me to call one of Barbra's assistants to see what the holdup was since Barbra had a deal with the photographer to approve any images that went to the magazine. After explaining to her assistant the urgency of the situation—that if we didn't get the photos by a particular date, we were not going to make the cover—she lit into me like I had just made the most outrageous request in the world.

"The photographer has the photos, and when he's done retouching them, that's when you'll get them!" the assistant screamed. Then she hung up on me. She was so out of control, I was shaking when I got off the phone. After John found out what had happened, he, too, went into a rage.

"Give me the phone. I'm calling her right now," John said. "How dare she talk to you like that!"

I appreciated his desire to defend me but wouldn't let him make the call. "That would be giving her a big ole gift," I said. "After screaming at me, she gets a call from John F. Kennedy Jr.? No way."

Ever the protective older brother, John also wasn't a fan of my new boyfriend, Joey. He thought I needed someone more mature and sophisticated—and he was right—but it was his fault we got together in the first place. Joey was the assistant to the creative director of Naked Angels, one of John's charities, and would often call the office to schedule board meetings. After we had spoken on the phone a few times, he told me he was in a band.

"Hey, if you're not doing anything tomorrow, why don't you come see us play at Brownies?" he said.

"Maybe."

"Great. Can you also tell John my band is playing?"

He had about as much chance of John Kennedy showing up at one of his gigs as he did John Lennon.

I didn't go to the gig and didn't meet Joey in person until John asked me to give him some direction in his hunt for a new job, since his boss had left Naked Angels. I put him in touch with some executives at Hachette, and as a thank-you, he asked me to lunch. We met for sushi across the street from the office, and—there's no other way to put it—he was fucking gorgeous. With his unruly, dark, curly hair that hung down to the middle of his back and huge blue eyes, I could hardly focus on food.

Joey was sweet, funny, and even a little shy. Despite my clear attraction to him, I put the idea of dating him out of my mind. There was no way that this kid in a rock band wasn't going out with nineteen-year-old groupies. He was just a nice guy repaying a favor with lunch.

That Sunday, though, he called to ask if I wanted to see his friend's band. I still didn't see it as a date; I figured he was playing it smart, staying in touch with me because of my proximity to John. If we became friends, maybe John would eventually show up at one of his gigs. So without expectation, I headed out that night with my own agenda of meeting new people—perhaps even someone as cute as Joey.

Waiting for me outside the club on Great Jones Street, Joey wore a thin blue Adidas T-shirt with white trim and had cut his hair so that the black curls ringed his face like an angel's—a really, really hot angel. He said with a deep, raspy voice, "Hey, baby, you look beautiful." His greeting took my breath away— my first crush at thirteen called me "baby," and I thought it was the sexiest thing a guy could say. Joey put his arm around my waist and tucked my hand into his back pocket. It was definitely a date.

Not many people had showed up at the venue, Under Acme, a dark box with low ceilings and black brick walls, where every band with loud music attempted to become the next Nirvana. The empty expanse of dance floor left Joey, me, and our obvious chemistry way too exposed.

"Wanna get out of here?" he asked after one song.

We ran up the stairs and several blocks to 9th Street, where we crashed directly into the heady scene at Café Tabac. We talked and laughed, but mostly we made out. We kissed for hours—next to the pool table, in corners, and on various couches—until five o'clock in the morning. The place was closing and the sun was coming up. I hailed a cab, and as I opened the door to get in, Joey said, "Where are you going?"

"I'm going home," I said.

"Can I come home with you?"

"No, let's save something for next time."

Joey was shocked, but he sort of loved it, too. He called the next day and every day after that. Whenever we saw each other, we both burst into big smiles, and then started kissing. We heard "get a room" called out on the street more times than I could count.

A couple of weeks after we began seeing each other, I went to one of his band's gigs and brought along two friends, eager to show off my sexy new boyfriend. The band had played only a few songs when the lead singer said into the microphone, "So, everybody, what do you think of Joey's new haircut?" The crowd cheered and I smiled, thinking about how his thick black hair felt in my hands. Then Joey leaned into the mic and announced, "I did it to get more pussy."

"Nice," my friend said.

"Well," I replied. "It's working."

Good-looking, young, and surrounded by groupies, Joey was a dangerous type to fall for. To add to that lethal combo, his parents were well-off. He had arrived in New York from an affluent Boston suburb. I'd seen his kind before: though he lived in a dive on the Lower East Side, he had no problem buying five-hundred-dollar Elvis Costello–style glasses or a good meal (using his dad's Amex). He acted poor, but his style and alma maters were too expensive for him to pull off an accurate portrayal.

No, Joey didn't exactly have *stability* written all over him. But I kind of got off on having the attention of a guy tons of girls gawked at every night. Still, I had to establish some kind of power, so I made him wait a month before sleeping with him. Joey turned my game into evidence of his desirability. "I know why you're not sleeping with me," he teased for the duration of that long month. "It's because you really like me."

I finally gave in to the inevitable at his apartment on Orchard Street, the vilest tenement I'd ever seen. It didn't even have a bathroom: the toilet was in the kitchen next to the stove, and he brushed his teeth and shaved at a sink filled with dirty dishes. I wouldn't touch a glass in that place. But that's where we had great sex for the first time. Unfortunately, the fun was short-lived, ending when Joey rolled over in bed and said, "You know, dude, I don't really want a girlfriend."

Just what every girl wants to hear right after having sex for the first time with a guy she likes. I got dressed and ran out of his apartment faster than I would have if the place were on fire.

I was exhausted and humiliated the next day when Joey casually called to say hi. He was completely surprised that I was upset and had no idea what he'd done.

"Uh, you told me you don't want a girlfriend," I reminded him.

"I never said that," he replied.

I let Joey convince me that I was overreacting, so I could stay in a relationship where we spent *a lot* of time making out and having sex. He worked two blocks from *George*'s offices, so we met downstairs around lunchtime almost every day to kiss and talk. In addition to great chemistry, we had great conversations—and there wasn't a lot of that going on in the Under Acme scene. "I feel like a chick, I talk so much around you," he'd say. Joey lavished me with compliments, telling me I was smart and had a stripper's body. "You're the coolest girl-friend I ever had," he said.

Joey fit into a larger pattern I had of surrounding myself with good-looking guys. That included not only men I had dated but also my male friends. Frank was so gorgeous that even John remarked on "how handsome" he was the first time they met. Also everyone, John included, had a crush on Matt Berman, but I'm the one who became his best friend in the office. And obviously there was John.

It doesn't take a shrink to figure out that I unconsciously gravitated toward good-looking guys as proof that I wasn't as unattractive as I felt. If I could date a guy as attractive as Joey, I couldn't be that bad-looking. That search for validation in others proved unfulfilling: it seemed that, no matter how much weight I lost, how nice my clothes were, how blond I got, or how cute my boyfriend was, I couldn't manage to feel good about my looks.

Several months into my relationship with Joey, he and I spent a weekend in Saratoga and Lake George. We hiked all day, then went out for dinner at a nearby pub. Over chicken and mashed potatoes, Joey told me how happy he was to have such a great girlfriend. *Me.* By the time I dropped him off at his apartment Sunday night, I was happy, too. I was falling in love.

That night, I lay in bed thinking about the next milestone in our relationship: Joey was going to spend Thanksgiving with my family. This was big—I hadn't brought anyone home in a few years. My family was loud and ethnic, probably nothing like Joey's liberal, Jewish neurosurgeon dad and fine-painter mom. I pictured my dad telling Joey how much he admired the Jews because "they stick together." I shut out that nightmare by thinking about my mother's out-of-this-world feast. She was an amazing cook—her food would counterbalance any political incorrectness on my dad's part. Joey's visit would be fine.

The anticipation mounted until a couple of days before the holiday, when, after an ordinary Friday-night date of dinner and a movie, Joey, propped on his elbow in bed and wearing the same Adidas shirt from our first date, told me he'd met another girl.

"I don't know if I like her, but I want the freedom to find out."

Joey never made it to Thanksgiving dinner.

I was devastated by the breakup, even though I recognized my hand in the situation. I said I wanted to find love in a real relationship, but I hadn't exactly picked the best candidate. I should have gone after a balding lawyer, not a hot rocker with girls slipping him their numbers every night.

I kept up my resolve to quit him, but a few weeks later, he began leaving voice mail messages at home and work, pleading for me to call him ("Call me back just so I know you're okay"). When he sent me flowers at the office a few days before Christmas, I caved. "I miss you and I think I made a mistake," the note read. When John saw who had sent the bouquet, he made his opinion known. "Are we going to get rid of that guy, or what?" he said.

The answer was no. I called Joey and invited him to a Knicks game the night before Christmas Eve. John had given me a pair of tickets for his amazing courtside seats—the kind where you're cheering next to Woody Allen or Spike Lee—and I wanted to impress Joey. It would be such an awesome night that he would ditch whoever he was dating and we'd get back together.

Our chemistry was still strong; we met at his apartment at the start of the evening and almost missed the game. As we sat down with our feet literally touching the court, Joey said, "I hope they don't put us on the JumboTron." I ignored his remark, thinking, *He'll come around.*

At the end of the night, Joey announced he had a Christmas gift for me, and my heart beat fast with the thought that maybe this was a pronouncement of some kind. I ripped open the lumpy, manhandled wrapping paper. Inside the little package was a brass Zippo lighter. Okay, not exactly diamonds or perfume, but all hope was not lost: there was a card—perhaps it held a meaningful, romantic sentiment. I read the one line: "Best of luck in the New Year, Joey."

Best of luck?

On the phone with Carolyn the next day, I went off: "Who fucking says, 'Best of luck in the new year'?"

"Why don't you ask John?" she said.

"What do you mean?"

"When we first started dating, John called me and, right before he got off the phone, said, 'Don't be a stranger.' I was so pissed I called him right back and said, 'Don't you ever say something like that to me again.'"

Of course, for Carolyn, that worked. Her demands were met because John was respectful and a real man. Joey was a stoner who had to stop at home to smoke pot before we went to dinner and often called me "dude."

Yet that didn't stop me from giving it one last try when he called again on Valentine's Day. Carolyn, whom I had tortured with Joey stories, begged me not to call him back. "Don't do it," she said. "Let him feel what it's like to be lonely." I tried my best, but it was goddamn Valentine's Day. The holiday of hearts and flowers put fantasies in my head: maybe he was serious this time and had finally realized the error of his ways. I called his apartment and got the answering machine. My pulse quickened at the sound of his voice. "You've reached Joey and Lisa's apartment, please leave a message." I froze. What the fuck was wrong with me? Why was I so stupid when it came to men?

Carolyn later offered her own analysis while we engaged in one of our favorite activities: drinking white wine and smoking on the couch in John's Tribeca loft, which she had moved into after *George*'s launch in September 1995. "Falling in love would be like jumping off a cliff for you," she said.

I didn't find her words terribly encouraging. Who wants to be told that it'll be hard for you to ever find love?

"Really, truly falling in love means trusting someone," Carolyn said. "And the person you trust most in the world, Rosie, is yourself."

She was right. I didn't really trust anyone. Though Joey didn't do much to change that fact, it wasn't entirely his fault. I kept the cycle of makeups and breakups going, as if I could will the relationship to work. But Carolyn didn't bullshit. Just as she didn't tolerate my putting myself down, she couldn't accept Joey's poor treatment of me.

"You are never going to end up with Joey," she said. "You need someone who is smart, funny, and most of all, somebody who you respect." Carolyn poured me another glass of wine and said, "No relationship is perfect. John and I have our fights. You know how inconsiderate he can be."

John's insensitivity was the biggest catalyst of their arguments. Carolyn would decline invitations from friends because John said he was coming home for dinner. So she would wait and wait and wait, while he worked late and went to the gym (without letting her know), and then waltzed into the apartment way past dinnertime. Carolyn was not only angry but also worried about him, which she had a right to be. Another classic scenario was when he would spring important information on her at the last minute, such as "Oh, by the way, the Whitney benefit is in two days" or "I'm bringing home a friend for dinner . . . right now." She wanted to know why the hell he didn't tell her sooner. It wasn't mean-spiritedness on his part. He was simply as disorganized and clueless as a kid. Still, it didn't make scrambling to accommodate him any less frustrating.

"Sure, I want to kill him sometimes," she said. "But I respect him."

Things could get really heated between them; for example, he would go crazy when she was on the phone all day while he was trying to get through, getting busy signal after busy signal since they didn't have call waiting; or it upset him when Carolyn, a big-sister type to many people, would spend an entire week dealing with someone else's problems, which took her attention away from John. But no matter the issue, John and Carolyn always defused the situation with a joke. They never took anything so seriously that they couldn't laugh at themselves. That, combined with the respect Carolyn had for John (and vice versa), took their relationship from dating to seeing each other three nights a week to living together within a year. The evolution was natural—and completely unlike my tortured dating life. It was hard to believe, but John and Carolyn were the normal ones.

CHAPTER

5

The press reported—over and over, well into their marriage— that when John asked Carolyn to marry him, she didn't immediately say yes, as if there were strife in their relationship. But that's not at all what happened.

When Carolyn called me on Monday morning after the Fourth of July weekend of 1995, she sounded like a little kid with an incredible secret.

"Rosie, are you ready for this?" she asked.

They had been at his house on Martha's Vineyard for the long weekend, just hanging out, when John suggested they go fishing. "I wanted to go fishing like I wanted to cut off my right arm," she said, laughing. But Carolyn agreed; she was always a good sport when it came to John's activities—kayaking, scuba diving, ice climbing, she was game.

"He asked me to marry him out on the water, on the boat,"

she said. "It was so sweet. He told me, 'Fishing is so much better with a partner.'"

"That's amazing!" I said.

"Yeah, but I've been a nervous wreck ever since I got off that boat. We had people up for the weekend, and I had to pretend like nothing happened. I just don't want anyone to know yet," she said. In her voice, I could hear the jitters stemming from her excitement and also from her nervousness over how people would react when they found out.

From the start, Carolyn was worried that when their engagement went public, the media would tear into her—saying she wasn't good enough for John. And she was right to worry, because that's exactly what happened.

I stopped by their apartment later that night and she showed me the ring, a platinum band surrounded by diamonds and sapphires. As soon as I saw it, I realized: *That's the secret package I picked up for John!*

A couple of months earlier, he had casually asked me to pick something up at Maurice Tempelsman's office. I assumed it was a gift for Carolyn, and I knew it had to be jewelry, because Maurice, who was Jackie Onassis's longtime companion until she died, was a diamond dealer. But John was so nonchalant, it didn't occur to me that I was picking up an engagement ring.

On the way out of Maurice's office, I put the box into a plastic Duane Reade bag so as not to draw attention to it, then hopped in a cab back to the office. I certainly wasn't getting on the subway carrying an expensive diamond something-or-other.

As soon as I got back to the office, I handed the Duane Reade bag to John, who put it in a drawer, where it remained for almost a week. I regularly went into his desk drawers, and it drove me nuts to see that plastic bag just sitting there. I imagined him throwing away the bag by mistake and saying, "It was in *that* bag?" I was relieved the ring had made it safely onto Carolyn's finger. A replica of an emerald and sapphire Schlumberger ring John's mother had owned, it was not a typical engagement ring. But it was simple and beautiful.

Despite all the time we spent together, John and I never had a direct conversation about his engagement. After Carolyn called me to deliver the news, I knew him well enough not to race into his office and shout, "Congratulations!" In fact, I knew not to bring it up at all unless he did first, which he didn't.

As far as he was concerned, news of the engagement was relegated to "girl talk," and he wanted no part of it. He assumed, correctly, it was something Carolyn would tell me during one of our dozens of daily calls. It became clear that I knew when he came home and found Carolyn and me on the couch sipping wine and talking about her anxiety over their engagement becoming public knowledge. "Oh, brother," he said. "Is this all we're going to talk about?" That was typical John, avoiding drama.

If there was any ambivalence about their getting married, it was on my part. Although I was happy for them, I was also slightly bummed. It had nothing to do with them, and everything to do with marriage. Couples were never as fun once they got married. People said, "I do," and then turned serious and boring. I hoped that wouldn't happen to John and Carolyn, because I really liked hanging out with them.

The three of us went to dinner with Frank once in a while, but mostly I spent time with them individually. I liked having separate relationships with John and Carolyn, because each friendship brought me different things.

Carolyn and I became such good friends that we would see each other a few nights a week and share the intimate details of our lives—"girl talk," as John called it. Whenever John was traveling or was with his guy friends, we'd get together for dinner or drinks, usually bringing along a combination of my good friends, Frank and Michele, or hers, Gordon and Jessica. Soon enough our friends started hanging out separately from us, which only strengthened my connection to Carolyn.

John and I mainly saw each other at the office, where we worked long hours (most days, eating two out of three meals at our desks). While I socialized more with Carolyn, my relationship with John had grown outside *George*. He was always my boss, but we also did things that Carolyn wasn't into, such as going to a Rolling Stones concert or a rehearsal for *Saturday Night Live*.

Whether I was talking about politics and current events with John, or Prada and Brad Pitt with Carolyn, most of my waking hours were spent with them. I worried that, once married, they would do everything together, changing the dynamic between the three of us that had become such a significant part of my life.

Carolyn was also worried marriage would change everything. She understood that the formality meant something, especially to John and his lifestyle; he was pretty old-fashioned, and given his place in the world, he couldn't be single forever. But she could have stayed engaged to and living with him indefinitely. Marriage came with obligations—familial, societal, even work-related—that had nothing to do with their relationship. As John's girlfriend, she could skip a benefit or advertiser dinner without her absence being considered an insult. Once she was his wife, everything would have to be more carefully considered and planned. And she still felt too young to deal with all that pressure.

She wanted to enjoy the bubble of privacy surrounding her engagement, however long it might last. That's why, in the beginning, she was nervous about going out in public with her ring. It had nothing to do with hesitancy over getting married and everything to do with privacy. But as time went on, she loosened up, wearing it on her right ring finger and saying it was simply a gift from John.

The bubble burst the Friday before Labor Day, when Carolyn called me early in the morning at my apartment after the *New York Post* ran a story about their engagement. The image of Carolyn had an inset blowup of her left hand, with the diamond and sapphire band circled for maximum effect. The story had an anonymous "good friend" confirming that they were getting married. I knew John and Carolyn had told only their closest confidants, and one of them had opened their mouth.

"What do you think we should do?" Carolyn asked.

"Nothing."

"Really?"

"No comment, as usual," I said.

But when I got into the office later that morning, it was

anything but business as usual. Behind the closed door to John's office, I could hear Michael freaking out. "This is going to take the thunder away from *George*."

The official launch of *George,* with a massive press conference, was less than a week away. Michael was very concerned that the news about John's engagement would eclipse their new magazine. Every single question would be about John's getting married, while *George* would be a footnote buried at the end of the story.

"How did she let this get out?" Michael said, opening the office door and pacing between my desk and John's.

"Who cares?" John says. "This is my life. I'm going to do what I've always done—ignore it and move on."

Tensions were high as John and Michael continued to yell at each other. A lot was at stake. Meanwhile, Carolyn called me repeatedly to find out what was going on. It was a tug-of-war—John and Carolyn on one side, not wanting to break with their protocol of silence when it came to dealing with the press, and Michael on the other, arguing that these were special circumstances.

I slunk down in my chair as Michael and John hashed out a solution behind his closed office door. There was no other way around it: the rumor had to be addressed before the press conference, and the only way to do that without setting off a firestorm of unwanted attention was to deny the engagement.

Nobody was happy about the situation. John was completely unused to addressing his personal life in public, and both he and Michael were uncomfortable about lying to the media. It was a gamble, but Michael saw it as their best option.

They finally opened John's office door, and Michael emerged holding a draft of the denial.

"If we are doing this, it can't come from me," he said. The person who issues a press release is often just as important as the contents of the release. It would have been weird for Michael, *George*'s publisher, to issue a statement about his business partner's personal life.

"Maybe it should come from the senator's office," John offered. They mulled the proposition of Ted Kennedy's team handling it, but in the end nixed the idea. John was now an editor in chief with his own staff. Having his uncle speak for him would have undermined his position.

Having it come from John was out of the question. And he didn't want the denial to come from anyone in PR, worrying that it would give the false impression that he retained a personal publicist.

Michael, standing in John's doorway, looked at me and said, "Maybe we should just have Rose do it."

I quickly made myself busy at my desk. I didn't know if he was serious, but I was nervous; my mind raced with the implications of issuing a statement to the press on John's behalf. On one hand, speaking publicly for John was a tremendous responsibility. On the other, if bombarded with questions and calls, would I get flustered and say something I shouldn't? One thing I knew for sure: if I fucked up, it would be a big blunder.

Michael and John stood for a moment considering the idea. I could feel their eyes on me, and looked up. Michael continued talking about me like I wasn't there, reasoning that I wasn't a publicist, so it would come off as a simple response from John's assistant, rather than a managed affair. John nodded pensively, and they continued to discuss me as they walked away. As soon as they were out of earshot, I picked up the phone and called Carolyn.

"*Now* what's going on?" she asked.

"I don't know. I think Michael wants me to issue the denial," I said, trying to sound nonchalant.

I felt doleful calling her with these details. She wasn't psyched about John publicly refuting their engagement, and going ahead with the charade would inevitably create a weird split between their real identity as a couple and their public image. The person who Carolyn woke up to every morning now had to say to the world that he wasn't marrying her. Such an announcement would undoubtedly taint what should have been an extraordinary phase of their relationship.

"I want it to come from you," Carolyn said. "If anyone is going to make a statement about my personal life, it should be you. You're the only one I fucking trust."

Knowing I had Carolyn's blessing kept me from passing out when John and Michael gave me simple instructions to fax the statement to the Associated Press that afternoon.

"What should I say if people call?" I asked nervously.

"Just read the statement," Michael said. "And tell them there's nothing more than what's in the statement."

I nodded. I had issued press releases at PR/NY, but nothing like this. Just my asking what I should say *if* people called revealed that I didn't comprehend the significance of the moment, or perhaps I was willfully in denial of what the next twenty-four hours would entail. I told myself I would fax this brief release, which would appear in the paper, and we would all return to life as usual.

The staff had emptied out of *George* early in anticipation of the holiday weekend, leaving for fun in the Hamptons, Connecticut—anywhere but here. John led the charge, giving me a quick, tense "thank you" before heading out the door. Just like with the wallet he had neglected to bring to the airport, once the problem was out of his hands, John wanted to forget about it. Despite the interior monologue that accompanied my nod of acknowledgment—*No, thank* you. *Have a great weekend! Don't worry about me, I'll be fine. Really*—I understood that he had flown past me because he felt awkward about the whole situation. When John wasn't 100 percent behind something—as was the case with addressing his private life—he didn't want to deal with it. He felt aggrieved not only because he was breaking protocol but also because of Carolyn. It sucked that he had to lie to the world about *this*.

Michael was the last to leave the office, stopping by my desk to wish me a good weekend and good luck. Shortly after, I checked the release for typos and hit send.

> Once again, John Kennedy seems to be bearing the brunt
> of a slow news day. The stories circulating regarding an
> engagement are untrue. He is not engaged. While it is
> not our habit to comment on John's personal life, this story
> seems to have taken on a life of its own, and we feel it
> necessary to respond.

I returned to my desk and waited for the calls to come. But nothing happened. Metaphorical crickets chirped as I sat there for almost an hour, at first surprised, and then pleased. *Cool, nobody cares.* And why should they on the Friday before the last long weekend of summer? It was a nonstory. I decided to leave. If I hustled, I might be able to salvage some of my weekend.

Until . . . the phone started ringing. At least a dozen calls came through within the first fifteen minutes once the barrage began. Reporters, like prosecutors, asked variations on the same question—Is John getting married? I answered rapid-fire, scared I would say the wrong thing.

"Are they engaged?"

"He's not engaged."

"What's the ring for?"

"It is just a gift. He's not engaged."

It was the same thing over and over.

"Are they planning to get engaged?"

"I don't know."

"Do they have any further comment?"

"No."

"Where are they going to be this weekend?"

"You have to be kidding me."

My friend A.J. Benza, who wrote a gossip column for the *Daily News,* called asking the same questions as all the other reporters. At least it was nice to hear a friendly voice. I met A.J. when I worked at PR/NY, and we bonded over the discovery that we were both Italian, were from the outer boroughs, and had a few friends in common. A.J. laid it on thick; he never missed an opportunity to seduce a female. Eventually we went out for a drink and became buddies. Now A.J., like any good columnist, tried to use his connections for a scoop.

"Come on, baby, how long have I known you?" he begged. "Just tell me if it's true. I'm not going to write it."

"A.J. Forget it."

When I finally got off the phone with him, I decided it would be best if I left the office. There was no point in my sitting there, picking up the phone, and setting myself up to say something stupid. Too paranoid to be incommunicado, I went directly home, where I opened the door tentatively, as if reporters were waiting for me inside. Instead, the quiet from the office had followed me home and now filled every inch of my studio. I immediately turned on the TV to find out what was going on and to kill the silence.

The evening news was in progress, and I sat through a political story and a crime tragedy before John's nonengagement news hit the airwaves. The anchor gave a classic lead-in to the story before the whole statement I sent out flashed on the screen with "RoseMarie Terenzio" at the bottom—*the entire statement*. I was shocked.

Statements are usually spliced and diced in the media, especially on television, where airtime is precious. But there it was in its entirety, my long, not particularly interesting statement. I realized then that everything I said about John had the potential to be big news.

In addition, after having kept my job secret for so long, everybody in the world now knew I worked for John. My parents and Frank knew about my job, but not many others did. No sooner had the statement aired than my phone started ringing off the hook.

"Oh my God. I just saw your name on the TV!" my mother yelled into the phone.

"Everybody's calling!" my dad said, grabbing the phone from her. "I'm so proud of you."

Soon *everybody* was calling, even girls I hadn't spoken to since high school. "Hi, this is Joanna. Remember me from your math class?" When I wondered how she'd found my number, Joanna answered, "Oh, your mom's giving it out."

I could deal with the mass media barraging me, but not my own family. My sister even asked if John would speak at my nine-year-old niece's school during career day. "Absolutely not," I said. "What's wrong with you, Anita!"

Finally I gave up and let the answering machine pick up all the incoming calls. The adrenaline began to wane, and a gloomy feeling took its place. The job could be lonely sometimes. Worse than John's empty office, the long string of vacated cubicles, or the silence of my studio, I was isolated by having to carry around confidential information. Everyone was so excited about the statement. Meanwhile, I knew it wasn't even true. Secrets became burdens, even if they were good ones. The only people I could talk to in depth about John and Carolyn were John and Carolyn—and that got boring after a while.

The red light on my answering machine blinked madly, as if it were a symbol of my inner turmoil. I had to get out of my own head. On the next ring, I threw caution to the wind and picked up the phone without screening. Big mistake.

"Hi, Rose, I saw the thing on the news," said a woman I knew casually. "Oh my God."

"Yeah, I know, it's been kind of crazy. It's nice to hear from you. Sorry it's been a while, but I kind of have to go . . ."

"Listen, the reason I'm calling is, I need one more person

in my wedding party. Rose, would you be in my wedding?"

I couldn't even speak. Be in her wedding? I hadn't seen this person in over a year.

"And maybe you could bring John as your date," she added.

If I thought people were crazy before, now that the secret of what I did for a living was finally out, I realized they were totally insane.

CHAPTER

6

My outfit was so gorgeous, it deserved its own press conference. For the official launch of *George,* I wore a pink suit handmade expressly for me. I couldn't believe I had a custom-made suit. (*I have people who make me things?*) And it wasn't made by just anybody. Lars Nord—the backstage tailor for all the big fashion shows, such as Oscar de la Renta, Versace, and Calvin Klein—had created the pencil skirt and cropped jacket, which fit perfectly. I met Lars after buying my first really expensive pair of pants; Carolyn intervened before I hemmed them. "Honey, you're not taking those to the dry cleaner," she said. "You need Lars." I quickly became friends with the Swedish tailor, who, incidentally, closely resembled Sting.

On September 7, 1995, the day of the launch, I took a taxi from my apartment downtown to Wall Street, because the white patent-leather stiletto mules I had chosen to complement the suit were not walking shoes.

I arrived so early that Federal Hall—the site of the first capitol of the United States, George Washington's inauguration, and the *George* press conference—was empty except for a few people running around doing last-minute tasks, like making sure the larger-than-life posters of the magazine's pages were correctly placed around the soaring columns. Only three days after successfully killing the story of Carolyn and John's engagement, I wanted to make sure I did everything I could to help the launch go smoothly, like double-check that John and Michael had the final copies of their speeches and special guests found their correct seats.

Once we opened the doors, nearly three hundred reporters, cameramen, and photographers rushed in, frenzied as they jockeyed for position. I had never seen that many cameras in one place. One would have thought the excitement was over Mideast peace being achieved, not the launch of a magazine. Of course, the media was there for John, but with my spending day in, day out by his side, it was easy to forget the scope of his popularity. Not in a million years did I think that this much media would show up, even for him.

I wasn't the only one surprised by the attention. Matt Berman was walking toward Federal Hall thinking, *What the hell is going on, today of all days?* He was worried he'd be late to the press conference . . . until he realized the melee was *for* the press conference.

Other than John, Michael was probably the only *George* staff member prepared for the moment. He began the press conference by introducing John with a classic line that only Michael could have thought up: "Being John Kennedy's partner is like being Dolly Parton's feet. I'm sure they're perfectly nice, but they tend to get overshadowed."

Then came the main event. When John strode up to the podium, a DJ played "Movin' on Up." (I wanted him to walk in to "Don't Believe the Hype," but it was too obvious, so we played it on the way out.) You could hardly hear the music because of all the camera shutters clicking. It was insane that a bunch of cameras could be so loud.

Faced with the crowd's reaction to John, I started to get anxious, thinking, *I really don't want to be responsible for this kind of person.* The stakes of my job suddenly seemed very high, even more so than during the engagement experience over the weekend. It was like jumping off a tall rock. Don't look. Just jump.

As John started to speak, there was a collective pause. I think we were all nervous for him. I know I was. John, the master of last-minute planning, hadn't finished his speech until around 10 p.m. the night before. Paul Begala, Bill Clinton's former adviser, had lent his expertise and helped write the original draft, but John scribbled his own edits while rehearsing at the podium. But from his first joke ("I don't remember seeing this many of you in one room since the results of my last bar exam"), he put everyone at ease. If I had a shred of doubt about him, it disappeared with that speech. It wasn't just his clever and careful words but also his delivery. He spoke to the crowd as if he were sitting in his living room with friends.

When the conference was over, I walked away with a newfound respect for John. Wow, that guy had a lot of pressure on him, but he didn't let it show, not for one minute. Yes, he got help with the words on the page, but he made them his own so that not one note was false. If there had been one put-on, John would have caught it. Even the most cynical son of a bitch in the room was rooting for him by the end of that speech.

The press conference was just the beginning of *George*'s exciting and amazing start. With a record 175 ad pages, the first issue completely sold out its print run of 500,000 copies after hitting newsstands several days later.

Every paper, magazine, and TV news program—from the very serious and political to totally pop—was commenting on our magazine. They didn't all say good things, but at least they were talking about us. In editors' offices or around my desk, we had fun following the speculation (about the magazine's future, John's next move, why a certain piece or photo had been chosen), knowing we had the real story. Sometimes, sitting on the subway going into work, I felt like I was in on a big secret. I looked at everybody else on the train and thought, *I have the best job ever*. I hadn't even turned thirty yet, and I was working with JFK Jr. at the most intriguing magazine in the country, in what seemed like the absolute center of the universe. I couldn't imagine a better place to be.

Of course, John was the real center. And everyone—I mean absolutely everyone—wanted a piece of him. Not only did he have to do the PR rounds, appearing in print interviews or on talk shows such as *Larry King Live,* but after the press conference, the clamoring for his attention within the magazine heightened. After witnessing his power on the stage and with other members of the press, some of the editors who had previously been skeptical of John's abilities suddenly wanted his opinion on everything.

It was my job to figure out who really needed to see him and who didn't.

"Can I talk to John?" a staffer asked.

"Sure, can I tell him what it's about?"

"I can't really explain it to you."

All righty, then, just go right ahead and barge in while he's on the phone and sit on his lap, why don't you?

"Okay, well, he'll want to be prepared, so can you give me an idea?"

I engendered resentment from some people every time I said no. I was the dumb secretary on a power trip, who didn't understand how magazines worked. But no matter how brutal or condescending some of them could be, I still never opened that door.

I also had to be more vigilant than ever with the phone. Now that John and *George* were in the news nearly every other day, the already-heavy volume of calls became heavier. People took the magazine as a new excuse to seek John out ("Could he come accept an editor-of-the-year award?" "Will he speak about the state of journalism at our symposium?"). And of course, the less resourceful crazies now knew *George* was housed in Hachette's building.

Because of all that (and perhaps because of nostalgia for the start of this madness), I continued to answer the phone by saying "Random Ventures" the entire five years I picked up John's phone. It was a tribute to the beginning, a reminder to enjoy the ride. It was also a brilliant way to sniff out a person and get a sense of who was legit and who wasn't. If I had a nut on the phone, I could easily throw him off.

The only tricky issue was not throwing off important

callers—such as the many celebrities who called to speak to John directly about participating in the magazine. When Robert De Niro called the office (most stars called John themselves, instead of having their assistants do it), he was really confused when I said, "Random Ventures."

"Is this John Kennedy's office?" he said in a tentative but sexy voice.

"Who's calling?"

"Bob De Niro."

Holy shit.

"I'll pass you right through, Mr. De Niro."

Stars usually called about being on the cover of the magazine. The conceit for *George* was that the person featured on each cover had to be George Washington in some shape or form. Matt Berman had to be really creative to come up with differing concepts so the images didn't run together month after month. (My personal favorite was Howard Stern as Washington chopping down the cherry tree.) De Niro, who was promoting *Casino* at the time, portrayed Washington with a Las Vegas touch. In the gorgeous photo, the actor is holding a sword with a playing card on the tip. Eventually, John and Matt agreed to include other political icons, since there are only so many George Washington cover ideas.

With the field opened up, it became a game among *George* staffers to make a clever match of current celebrities with historical figures. We would sit in each other's offices, thinking about our favorite personalities and concepts that would make sense for the magazine, convince John, and please the celebrities. To his credit, John went for some way-out ideas. When Matt suggested Kate Moss as Eve, the first woman in the world, for the 20 Most Fascinating Women in Politics issue, it was out of left field. But John gave the go-ahead, and the cover of the naked supermodel concealing herself with one hand and reaching out to a snake with the other became an instant collectible.

The magazine looked so fresh and cool because we didn't have any preconceived ideas. Matt would pore over the images of every American reference possible—from the Iwo Jima statue to Rosie the Riveter—and sketch out elaborate drawings that pushed the boundaries of publishing. Sometimes John meandered into Matt's art room while he was working and made comments like "That looks weird" or "I've never seen hair like that." But Carolyn, one of Matt's biggest supporters, put a stop to his intrusions. "Leave Matt alone," she said, shooing John out. "Just let him do his thing." There was one idea Matt couldn't convince John to accept: his posing with Carolyn on the cover in an imitation of the famous painting *American Gothic.* "Are you kidding?" John said. "Things aren't so bad that I have to put myself on my own cover." The concept went out to Bruce Willis and Demi Moore, but they also declined.

We wanted celebrities we liked to pose for the cover, but we also tried to feature ones who would make news and sell magazines. Marlon Brando, one of the most elusive figures in Hollywood, who hadn't done any press in years, fit the bill perfectly. Dressing him up as bad Santa for the cover of the holiday issue would have been a huge get. The request was a long shot, but when John was doing the asking, there was always a possibility. John sent the reclusive actor a letter with no expectation of a response. Then one evening, while we were at the office late to close the magazine, I received a phone call.

"Random Ventures."

"I'm trying to reach John Kennedy" came the marble-mouthed reply.

"May I ask who's calling?"

"This is Marlon Brando."

The name jolted me upright. "Hello, Mr. Brando, hold on, I'll get Mr. Kennedy for you."

"Wait a minute, miss. Who are *you*? What's your name?"

"RoseMarie."

"RoseMarie what?"

"Terenzio."

"Do you speak Italian?"

"Yes, I do, Mr. Brando," I answered proudly. I was looking forward to impressing him with my fluent Italian.

"If I said to you, '*tu sé nu sfachim*,' what would you say?"

I wasn't expecting *that* kind of Italian. This was not a dialogue I was prepared to have.

"I would say that's not a nice thing to say to someone you don't know."

"Fair enough. Let me ask you a question: Have you ever been to Hollywood, RoseMarie?"

"I was only there for a week."

"Well, you should stay away. Know why?"

"No."

"Hollywood is a toilet bowl. It's the most disgusting place in the world. . . ."

As Brando continued to spiral into a litany of complaints against his hometown, I realized his reputation for being bizarre was totally understated. The conversation was so weird that

I started to worry about what was going to come out of his mouth next and nervously cut him off.

"Hold on, Mr. Brando. I think Mr. Kennedy is anxious to speak with you."

I ran into John's office. "It's fucking Brando on the phone."

"Wow, all right. Put him through."

John was shocked that the famous recluse had responded to his letter. And, after talking to Brando, John was more shocked at the depth of his insanity. The actor agreed to the cover shoot, but only on one condition: that he could interview John on camera and pitch it as a TV special. Needless to say, John did not agree to his terms, and the cover offer went to Jack Nicholson instead.

Although just a small part of what I did at *George,* manning those phones was a full-time job—one that John was more than willing to help out with. Many times I would return from the bathroom or from grabbing something for lunch to find John sitting on my desk with the phone in the crook of his neck.

"Random Ventures," he said. "No, she's not here right now."

"Someone called for you, Rosie."

"Who was it?"

"I don't know. I didn't take a message."

Answering the phone gave him a thrill. He absolutely loved it. Still, if you're going to do a job, you've got to do it right. "If you aren't going to take a message," I scolded him, "then don't pick up the phone. How would you like it if I didn't take a message for you?"

I remember girlfriends calling and saying, "Some guy answered when I called earlier."

"It was John."

"Shut the fuck up. It was not."

"Yes, it was him. He loves playing receptionist."

I understood the appeal of the mundane task: it offered John an escape, a rare moment of anonymity. He was at the height of his fame now that he had launched a magazine at the heart of the cultural conversation. Wherever he and *George* went, everyone else wanted to follow.

Especially when we had a party.

Waiting outside the Art Institute of Chicago for John to arrive for the *George* party at the 1996 Democratic National Convention, I could only think, *What have we done?* On the steps, a million amped-up paparazzi, protestors, and gawkers congregated to get a glimpse of John and other celebrities, such as Arnold Schwarzenegger, Hillary Clinton, Oprah Winfrey, and Chris Rock.

After the invitations for the party went out, the office phones didn't stop ringing for days. People went nuts trying to get on the list, begging and offering bribes: a weeklong stay at a four-star hotel, a year's supply of haircuts, cases of champagne, new clothes, money. Despite our efforts to keep the number of guests down, it ballooned from a couple of hundred to more than a thousand in what promised to be the hottest event at the convention. And now I was sweating the reality of the mob.

When John arrived, the crowd went wild, waving posters, shouting, and beeping car horns, as if they were at a parade. Flashes from cameras, personal and professional, lit up the night. He hopped out of the car, debonairly buttoned his jacket, and in a few confident strides, stood next to me.

"Hey, Rosie," he said as if we were headed to the movies or something equally ordinary. "You look nice."

I smiled but was dying inside with worry that John was going to hate this huge, unruly party—and *me* for not being able to control it. "John, this is crazy," I said, right before we walked through the doors.

"This is exactly what we want," he said. "We're the biggest game in town tonight."

The museum's enormous hall was so packed it felt claustrophobic. And John instantly became the center of the sea of people. News of his arrival spread through the building like wildfire, and everyone tried to move closer to him. They wanted photos or a word or, worse, to touch him. I clutched his arm in alarm and started pushing through the mob scene, yanking young women away.

I'd never seen a crowd swarm one person and follow him throughout a building. There were far too many people (and the people were way too into it) for me to offer any real protection. Partygoers started jumping over one another to get a photo. *If this crowd turns, we're dead in one second,* I thought.

"Are you okay?" I asked John.

"Yup."

The two hours that John spent doing rounds at the party were some of the worst of my life. I had worn a spaghetti-strap dress, and the morning after the event, my back was covered in bruises from where I was poked and prodded.

By the time Hillary Clinton and Senator Ted Kennedy showed up to the museum, fire marshals were right on their heels. We had broken every code in the book, and they were going to shut down that shit show.

The marshals were distracted long enough for the in-house party photographer to get a shot of Hillary, Teddy, and John together. After the picture was snapped, John left and the fire officials closed the party.

But they needn't have bothered. As soon as John walked out, the crowd completely died down. It was nearly instantaneous. I don't know how or why, but people could sense that he was gone. It was as if Elvis left the building and nobody cared anymore.

As soon as the party ended, the fun started for me. Because of my job, I had tickets to the best events that weekend (even standing near a newly skinny Oprah at one point).

I had gone from being a nobody who rode the express bus into Manhattan from the Bronx to someone with a pass to places and parties where even the rich and powerful were denied entry. The A-list treatment I received as John's personal assistant was astounding—and addictive.

Nothing was off-limits, from a VIP pass for the vice president's convention speech to Versace shoes. Even when I broke my favorite heels—black patent-leather Versace sling-backs with an embossed lace pattern that Carolyn had bought for me—I had a solution, thanks to my proximity to John.

I thought the shoes were destroyed after the heel broke while I was dancing to Stevie Wonder (live) at a benefit for the Robin Hood Foundation. One of the Lucite heels cracked, revealing the metal rod at its center. I tried to reattach the broken piece myself with Krazy Glue, but when I put weight on the heel, the piece became dislodged again. I brought it to my local shoe guy, who shook his head no; then to one of the fancy midtown shoe-repair places that service the Manolo

Blahnik set. I was ready to pay through the nose, anything to get those beauties back. But no, they confirmed, the heel couldn't be fixed.

Heavy with sadness and resignation (I'd had a lot of fun in those heels), I tucked the shopping bag holding the shoes under my desk. But I couldn't let go. I had one more idea. I decided to call the PR department at Versace.

"Hi, it's RoseMarie from John Kennedy's office," I said. After explaining my predicament, I asked, "Is there any way you can fix my shoe?"

"Unfortunately, we can't fix it. And we don't carry that style anymore. I'm so sorry," the person said. "You can go to the Fifth Avenue store and pick out any pair of shoes you want as a replacement. I'll call ahead and let them know you're coming, RoseMarie."

"Really?"

"It's the least we can do."

"Okay. Thanks!"

It was ridiculous. I could call anyone on the planet, and all I had to say were those seven magic words—"Hi, it's RoseMarie from John Kennedy's office"—and not only would I get right through or receive a call back, but the person would move heaven and earth to help me. Fashion houses, restaurant owners, club promoters, movie publicists. Anyone.

I quickly learned to use John's influence to get into the best locales in the city, such as Moomba, the restaurant and lounge where media moguls, models, and movie stars made the news that filled the gossip pages the next day.

Although John was never going to step foot in Moomba (Jennifer Lopez, Gwyneth Paltrow, or Puff Daddy bouncing to house music wasn't exactly his scene), the club's publicist Lizzie Grubman was always cool with me. I never had trouble skipping the line of hopeful partiers outside the downtown hot spot, even when the club hosted a special event for the Yankees shortstop Derek Jeter and first baseman Tino Martinez. I knew my niece, a rabid Yankees fan, would absolutely freak out if she could meet a few members of the team—especially Tino, her favorite. When the handsome baseball players gave her hugs and posed for pictures (even though they had no idea who we were), it was my niece's version of a Cinderella moment.

I never traded favors or made any promise of payback involving John when I accepted invitations, and I thought carefully before making personal requests, not wanting to compromise my boss's reputation. But when Pearl Jam came to town and sold out Madison Square Garden in about four seconds, I had to ask. They were one of my favorite bands, and I had never seen them live. I asked John if I could use his name to get tickets from the record company. "Yeah, I want to go, too," he said. "Get four tickets. But we have to pay for them." John and Carolyn never took anything—tickets, clothes, or dinner at a restaurant—for free.

"No problem," the rep at the record company said when I called. "Just fax me the request with the night you want to go and how many tickets you need."

Easy as dialing the phone, we got four tickets with backstage passes to the hottest concert in town. I invited my friend Gary and a *George* editor, a big Pearl Jam fan with whom I was at loggerheads, in an attempt at a truce. The fourth ticket was for John, who said he'd meet us at the concert, since he had an engagement earlier in the evening. I practically pinned his ticket to his lapel before he left the office that night, because I didn't want him to lose it.

The three of us went nuts when we got to our seats at the Garden. I had never been so close to any performance. I turned around to survey the crowd, and my heart stopped for a second: Joey sat three rows behind us. Trying to be mature, I went back to say a quick hi before the show started. He was in a relationship with Pearl Jam's manager—which might have ruined my night if his seats weren't behind mine. I had better seats. Awesome.

Pearl Jam did not disappoint. We rocked through the first set, and with each song I got more excited at the opportunity to meet the band's front man, Eddie Vedder, backstage. But three-quarters of the way through the show, John still hadn't arrived, and I didn't feel comfortable going backstage without him. So I left right after "Better Man," one of my favorite songs, to check my answering machine. There was a message from John: "Sorry, Rosie, I thought I could get there, but I can't. Hope you have a great time."

I returned to our seats and broke the news to the guys. My friend Gary might have been the only person who loved Eddie Vedder more than I did. But I absolutely could not say to Eddie, "Sorry, John F. Kennedy Jr. couldn't make it. But I'm his assistant, RoseMarie." Get out of here.

While I was just as disappointed as the boys that we wouldn't be coming in physical contact with a rock god, I would never dream of giving John a hard time about flaking. (Besides, he would have thought I was ridiculous for not using the backstage passes just because he couldn't make it.) Not only did my job offer all those amazing perks but, on top of that, John was incredibly generous to me.

When I casually brought up the idea of taking a vacation, he insisted I use his house in Hyannis for a week in August.

"Nobody will be there except for Provi," John said. "She makes amazing rum daiquiris with fresh lime."

Provi had worked for John's father when he was a senator, and then for his mom, so she was like part of the family.

"You can bring a friend," he said.

"Promise you won't show up?" I said, teasing.

I invited my best girlfriend, Michele Ammon, who was always up for an adventure. She couldn't get over our luck at scoring a free vacation. I was a little unsure about what to expect. Should I bring food and wine? What did people wear in Hyannis? Carolyn told me to chill out and not bring anything except my bathing suit.

When we arrived in Hyannis, Michele and I got lost for a while, tooling around in our rental car while searching for the gate to John's house. I don't know if we were expecting a big gold sign with *Kennedy* embossed on it or what, but the house didn't stand out in any way. It was a nice place, but very simple, with two small, cute bedrooms and a master bedroom upstairs and one bedroom downstairs, a cozy, warm kitchen, and a big porch out front—not unlike a typical beach rental for a normal family.

The real standout was Provi, a small, adorable Latin woman who was so spicy she immediately became part of our crew. Because she had been employed by the Kennedys for so long, I imagined her as an old lady we would have to tiptoe around. Instead, she was always up for a party.

When Michele and I returned in the afternoon from a

glorious day at the beach, rum daiquiris and a cheese plate were waiting for us on the porch.

"Okay, girls, time to shower and get ready for dinner," Provi said when we were done with cocktails.

Freshly showered and changed, we came downstairs to a magnificent meal of roast chicken, peppers, and rice—nothing opulent, but always a proper dinner with wine and cloth napkins. A sense of occasion perpetually surrounded the house in Hyannis.

After dinner, we went into the living room or outside on the porch to sit, talk, and sip our wine. We hashed out everything with Provi: current events, work, boys—you name it. Then we went to bed and did it all over again the next day.

Every summer, John would tell me, "Rosie, this is your week in Hyannis." Not only had I become someone who owned custom-made suits, now I vacationed on the Cape. I couldn't believe my good fortune.

John and Carolyn were effortlessly generous year-round, but Christmas was particularly overwhelming. The day before the holiday break was business as usual at *George*—for about five minutes. Everyone went into their offices, and then immediately shot back out, acting like six-year-olds on Christmas morning. Carolyn had spent a ton of time and money finding the perfect personal gift for each member of the staff. I tried to talk her out of it when she told me her plan, but she had gone ahead and scoured stores and catalogs for just the thing each person wanted: a top-of-the-line juicer for the vegetarian; an original print from the famous photographer Weegee for Matt Berman; engraved pens; beautiful handbags. Her perfectionism made for a lot of happy people.

The staff was comparing loot with big smiles on their faces when I heard John calling me.

"*Psst*. Hey, Rosie, get over here."

I walked over to my desk where he was watching the group.

"You going home for the holidays? 'It's a long way to Staten Island,'" he sang to the tune of "It's a Long Way to Tipperary."

"I'm not from Staten Island," I protested. "What are you doing? Do you have a coach riding you up and down Fifth Avenue for Christmas?"

John smiled and stepped aside to make room for me to sit at my desk, which was piled high with gifts from Carolyn. There were big boxes, little boxes, Barneys garment bags, and Miu Miu shopping bags. My mouth dropped open. This had to be some kind of joke. Or she'd lost her mind.

"You're such a brat, Rosie," he said. "You should be embarrassed by all those gifts."

John was kidding, but I *was* embarrassed and quickly stashed them away so I could open them later. John then handed me one more gift: a card.

"Merry Christmas, Rosie," he said.

"Merry Christmas," I said, taking the envelope and pulling out the card, which had a pig on it.

Inside the envelope was something else: a check. I had to look twice to make sure I was reading the number right. It was for five thousand dollars. I had never in my life seen so much money at one time.

I threw my arms around him. "I don't know what to say."

"You deserve it." John hugged me, and although I didn't believe him, I felt proud that I'd earned it by his estimation. John

To Rosey,
look familiar?
Here's a pant-load of
present because your a brat;
Love John + Carolyn.

didn't throw money around—he had a respectful relationship to it—so I must have done something right.

At my parents' house a day later, I couldn't wait to share my good fortune. Christmas was one of the only harmonious times in our house. In fact, our home during the holidays was the best place to be—safe and comfortable and full of the scent of an amazing feast cooking in the kitchen.

Christmas preparations started a month in advance, with my mom planning the menu for the twenty or so family members who often showed up for dinner (the only "outsider" ever invited for Christmas Eve dinner was Frank). After my mother had settled on her long list of dishes, she scoured the Italian grocery stores on Morris Park Avenue, smelling each fish suspiciously, tasting each hunk of cheese, squeezing tomatoes, haranguing owners for the freshest ingredients, and then revamping her menu to reflect the best she could buy.

The traditional Italian Christmas Eve meal of seven fish courses was challenging to prepare—even for someone as tough as my mom. Beginning a week beforehand, my mom made every single dish from scratch, with exacting standards that could drive a sous-chef/daughter crazy. But Christmas wasn't Christmas in the Terenzio household unless we went to mass at 6:00 p.m., followed by a late feast of shrimp and calamari in tomato sauce, baked clams, spaghetti with clam sauce, smelt pie, and so on.

I walked through the door the morning of Christmas Eve and immediately took in the aroma: the entire house smelled of fish. In the kitchen, my mom was hunched over the sink, shucking clams with a special knife. Newspapers covered the floor to soak up the fish juice that splattered during the intense preparations. The briny fragrance of a bowl filled with tiny silver fish—that my mother had spent hours cleaning—mixed with the tang of raw garlic on a cutting board and with the perfume of rich tomato sauce bubbling in a big pot on the stove.

After my mom leaned away from the sink to give me a kiss, I washed my hands and set to work. She shucked the clams and cut up the meat, and I combined the chopped-up clams with oregano, parsley, olive oil, and bread crumbs and stuffed the mixture into the cleaned shells.

"Not too many bread crumbs," my mom said to me more than once. "You want to taste the clams. Not too much."

With the clams in the oven, I slipped out of the kitchen. My dad was watching TV in his chair, and my heart squeezed at the big smile that spread across his face when I walked into the room. Life had never been easy for my parents, but the last couple of years were especially difficult. Having no money is hard. Having no money and getting old is harder.

I sat down in the love seat next to his chair, called my mom in from the kitchen, and handed him an envelope. "I want to give you guys my Christmas gift a little early," I said.

My dad looked up at me questioningly, and then took out the two-thousand-dollar check in his name. He said in Italian to my mother, "You can't believe what's in here.

"We can't accept this," he said, looking away and pushing the envelope into my chest. "This is your money."

"RoseMarie! This is crazy," my mom said. "You can't give us this kind of Christmas gift."

"You have to take this," I said. "After all the times you've struggled, I want you to have it for whatever you want to do."

Teary-eyed, my dad walked out of the room, returning after he'd taken a few moments to compose himself.

My mother looked at me and said, "RoseMarie, you don't pay your parents back."

"I'm not paying you back. I'm giving you a gift because I can afford it," I said. "Take it now, because it might not be here next year."

Working for John was the ride of a lifetime, never mind the fringe benefits—the invitations, the presents, the money. By his side, I sometimes got front-row seats to moments I only dreamed of witnessing. For me, the White House Correspondents' Association Dinner in the spring of 1999, the annual event at which politicians, journalists, and celebrities gathered for the rare chance to hear the president poke fun at himself and be teased by others, was just such a moment.

By that time, I had grown in my role as an assistant from one who answered phones and opened mail into something of a chief of staff, responding for John and strategizing his PR. Perhaps that's why I was emboldened enough to ask for a ticket to the dinner. I didn't like to ask John for favors, and this was a big one—both of which made me incredibly nervous about approaching him. *George* had purchased only a few tables, and the priority was to have political figures and celebrities sit at them, which meant very few seats were left for even the editors. It was a coveted invitation. Would it be unfair to the editors who couldn't go if I, an assistant, got to attend?

I didn't want to overstep, but I had discussed it with Carolyn and she felt that I had earned it. "You *have* to go," she said. Because of her anxiety over the scrutiny she would face at the dinner and the fact that she would feel more comfortable if I was there, I worked up the courage to make the outrageous request.

"John, is there any way I can go to the correspondents' dinner this year? I'll pay for my own hotel and my own ticket there."

"You can go, Rosie. And you don't have to pay for your ticket. If we can't find you a room, you can sleep on a mat outside our door."

I immediately called Michele with the amazing news.

"What's that?" she said. "Are you having dinner at the White House?"

"You know, I'm not entirely sure."

Wherever the dinner was held (not at the White House, I quickly learned) didn't really matter: from the dirty looks I got around the office from some staffers who were not going, I knew the evening would be every bit as incredible as I imagined.

After securing a ticket, the next thing I had to do was find an outfit worthy of wearing to see the president of the United States in person. Luckily, I had the best stylist in town—Carolyn, who encouraged me to pull a Sharon Stone and pair a billowing black organza skirt we found at BCBG with a simple black tank top from the Gap. When I tried on the whole ensemble at their place in Tribeca, Carolyn cooed, "Oh, honey, it's gorgeous . . . but wait." She scampered to her bedroom and came out bearing a necklace of three weighty rows of Indian rose-cut diamonds. The sparkling piece, a Christmas gift from the jeweler Maurice Tempelsman, was stunningly intricate, with red and gold enamel flowers covering the back of each diamond. She held it up to me.

"Oh no, Carolyn. I can't."

"You have to," she said, clasping the diamonds around my neck.

"No way. This necklace is terrifying. What if I lose it?"

"You're not going to lose it. How could you lose it? It's so big."

She twisted my arm, and I borrowed the diamonds—Carolyn was a very persuasive fairy godmother.

Getting together an outfit that included serious jewels was definitely like a fairy tale. But I returned to reality while wrestling with the logistics of *George*'s tables for the event. Working out seating arrangements is never fun. But when you're dealing with movie stars, incendiary publishers, and political insiders, it's a fucking nightmare.

Originally, *George* was set to host the actor Sean Penn, the conservative political commentator Ann Coulter, *Hustler* publisher and Clinton supporter Larry Flynt, the millionaire Republican newspaper publisher and Clinton hater Richard Mellon Scaife, the historian Douglas Brinkley, the king of the gonzo journalists Hunter S. Thompson, the actress Claire Danes, and longtime Clinton adviser Harold Ickes.

Unfortunately, Scaife, who had spent a lot of money trying to bring Clinton down after the Monica Lewinsky scandal, canceled a week before the dinner because he didn't want to sit at a table with Flynt, who had spent a lot of money trying to get women who had affairs with Republican leaders to come forward and expose their hypocrisy. Scaife's wife called and told me, "Dear, he's deaf as a post. He won't be able to hear anything in that place."

He wasn't the only last-minute dropout. Only two days before the dinner, Thompson also bowed out. Jann Wenner—the publisher of *Rolling Stone,* which had employed him for many years and originally printed his famous piece *Fear and Loathing in Las Vegas*—got wind of the plan and, John surmised, gave the writer an ultimatum: either you're at *Rolling Stone*'s table or you're not at anyone's table. As rebellious as Thompson could be, he wasn't an idiot. Through his assistant, he begged off because of a supposed fight with his girlfriend.

To add insult to injury, Thompson had insisted the magazine book him a two-bedroom suite at the Four Seasons, where people had booked rooms four months out and where everyone attending the dinner was staying. The exorbitant room was completely nonrefundable, and I had the thankless task of relating the news to John. But there was a silver lining: my hotel upgrade to Thompson's suite.

When I arrived in Washington, D.C., I took over the suite, which looked more like a gorgeous Upper East Side Manhattan apartment than a hotel room. There was no use in letting all that luxury go to waste. I wasn't the only one who got an upgrade. The Four Seasons had put John and Carolyn in the Presidential Suite, which with its living room, formal dining room, and three bedrooms made my accommodations look like the projects. I thought John was going to take my head off for allowing the upgrade.

"This is ridiculous," John said, while Carolyn sat curled up on the couch giggling.

"I didn't do it! They just saw your name," I protested. "What do you want me to do?"

John claimed he was worried that the suite was going to cost the magazine a fortune, which the correspondents' dinner already had, even though he knew it wouldn't. He was just embarrassed by the lavish display of attention.

After I talked him down, I returned to my room to get ready. Nothing could ruin my night—no last-minute cancellations or lodging dilemmas. I was determined to enjoy myself. The Washington Hilton's banquet hall, where the dinner took place, was filled with celebrities hobnobbing with journalists and political bigwigs. And the biggest celebrity of all was the president. Bill Clinton was in his element, warmly shaking hands with guests and leaning in for the occasional friendly comment. At first, I didn't know whether to get on the receiving line. Who the hell was I? But I had a ticket like everyone else and didn't know when I'd have another chance to meet the president.

When I finally stood face-to-face with him, I almost died. No matter your political affiliation, it's an honor and a privilege to meet the sitting president of the United States. You are in the presence of someone who commands respect for taking the hardest job in the world. Electricity ran through me when President Clinton shook my hand.

Arriving at the table where I was sitting with a handful of *George* staffers, I couldn't stop buzzing from my encounter with the president and almost missed John. Almost. He was walking in late behind the color guard, which was playing "Hail to the Chief," when we spotted each other from across the room. I didn't dare wave, not wanting to draw attention to him. John didn't have the same concern: he smiled and gave me the finger.

When he came over from his table, where he was hosting the celebrity guests, I gushed about meeting the president.

"I can't believe I'm in the same room as the president!" I said. "And I just shook his hand!"

A top editor, who had accompanied John from the other table, rolled his eyes. "Oh God, Rose. Do you know how many times I've been in the same room with the president? It's not that big a deal," he said, giving John a quick glance for approval.

His comment temporarily burst my bubble, a quick and piercing reminder that I didn't belong in that ballroom. But then, just as quickly, John turned it around.

"If you're so jaded, I don't really want you at my table. It *is* a big deal to be here," John said to the editor. "Rosie, you can take his place at my table."

He didn't have to say it twice. I grabbed my purse and left my empty spot at the table to the editor, as I headed off to enjoy an evening of pure magic.

Carolyn chatted with Claire Danes, who had brought her dad as her date. I sat next to Harold Ickes, and we fell in love for the night. Fascinated that I came from the Bronx, Clinton's former deputy chief of staff wanted to hear the whole story of how I met John and wound up sitting at the White House correspondents' dinner. And I adored him for his political genius and for listening.

Despite all the fun I was having, the night was still work.

I had to do a fair amount of the usual troubleshooting. Even though no photos were allowed and an astounding 2,700 people were in attendance, partygoers kept coming over to our table to snap pictures of John and Carolyn. I hadn't expected it from this crowd. After permitting a few fans to take pictures, when they kept snapping away like paparazzi, I stood up and said, "That's enough, now. We're all trying to enjoy the evening. Can you please respect their privacy?"

It pissed them off, and a few refused to stop, but I won in the end. Sean Penn, who sat at John's table, seemed to appreciate my tough antiphoto stance. He took a stand of his own that night. Inside the dinner, where smoking was prohibited, Sean flouted the rules by chain-smoking. At one point, a waiter came over and said, "Sir, there's no smoking in here." Looking lazily at the waiter, Sean said, "Well, what are you going to do? Arrest me?" And that was the end of it. He kept smoking, which meant we all got to smoke. So I thanked him by slipping another waiter a twenty to keep bringing Sean vodka tonics, despite the fact that they were serving only wine during dinner.

Toward the end of the evening, I slipped away from the table and found a pay phone in the lobby, hoping to make the historic moment real with a crucial call.

"Dad, I met the president tonight," I said into the phone.

If I could have chosen one person to sit next to me at that dinner, it would have been my dad. A lifelong political junkie, he thought riveting TV was a congressional debate on C-SPAN. "The son of a bitch is trying to bankrupt the country," he'd scream at the TV.

"Oh yeah, what was he doing?" My dad laughed on the other end. "What he does best—signing autographs?"

A staunch Republican, my dad particularly disliked the Democratic president, criticizing him for his arrogance and for exploiting his celebrity status. But my father did have respect for his position as leader of our country and what it meant for me to meet him.

"Marion," he yelled to my mom. "Can you beat this? Your daughter met the president tonight."

I could hear the pride in his voice and wanted to give him even more of a reason to be proud: "And John asked me to sit at his table during dinner."

"Well," my dad said, "John has good taste."

CHAPTER

7

———

John called me into his office one day in the early summer of 1996, and I could tell from the look on his face that he was up to something.

"Rosie, who's the most fascinating woman in politics?" He was working on ideas for the cover of *George*'s annual 20 Most Fascinating Women in Politics issue.

"Hillary Clinton?" I said.

"Yeah, okay. But she already said no to the cover. I've got another idea," he said, looking like the cat that swallowed the canary. "I think we should dress Madonna up as my mother. Wouldn't that be a riot? We'll have her in the pillbox hat, sitting on a stack of books."

"That's hilarious," I said, turning to get back to my desk, assuming it was just another inside joke.

"Great. Will you get your pad? I'm going to write her a note."

"Wait, you're serious?"

"Yeah. You thought I was joking?"

I had to give it to the guy. It took balls, and a pretty wicked sense of humor, to entertain such an irreverent idea. He picked Madonna because she was the most controversial figure in pop culture—and they had a friendship. She would acknowledge the concept and be as satiric about it as he was. John stood on a remarkably fine line between understanding the power of his family and not taking it seriously. Far from oblivious, he knew exactly what he was doing in terms of the magazine. John was able to separate his mom from the political icon Jackie Onassis. I thought the idea was cool, but I also worried about the reaction of the public, which didn't have the same ability to make that separation. Dressing Madonna as Jackie O could be the ultimate shit storm.

"Wow. Are you ready to take the heat for this?"

"If it doesn't bother me, why should it bother anyone else?"

"Okay, but you get what this will do, right?"

"Yes, Rosie. I totally get it. It will be fodder for every media outlet and probably most of my family."

"If you're in, I'm in. I think it's great because it's coming from you."

As it turned out, John wasn't the only one with a sense of humor. The day after we faxed a note to Madonna with the concept, she faxed back a message I'll never forget.

Madonna

dear Johnny boy
thanks for asking me to be
your mother but I'm afraid
I could never do her justice.
My eyebrows aren't thick enough
for one. when you want me to
portray Eva Braun or Pamela
Harriman I might say yes!
Hope you're well
love
Madonna

After Madonna said no, John dropped the idea (you had to do it all the way or not at all), but it became a little secret shared only with Matt Berman. We didn't tell anyone else about the outrageous idea—not even Carolyn, who would have killed him if he had gone through with it. She had enough scrutiny on her hands as it was.

The September cover wound up being almost as provocative: Drew Barrymore re-creating the notorious image of Marilyn Monroe singing "Happy Birthday, Mr. President" (with those words as a headline in case anyone didn't get it). Matt had

Mario Sorrenti shoot the actress and used a new color process that at the time was very arty and innovative. The strange hues were what kept Drew from looking cheesy or campy.

As expected, the media blasted John for the cover. He was skewered for being tasteless and exploiting a historical scandal to sell magazines. I could only imagine what the press would have said if Barbra Streisand, who was initially approached to pose as Monroe but turned it down, had agreed to the cover. If John couldn't play with political symbols, then he didn't belong in his job. He took it all in stride. Sure, he wanted to sell magazines; however, the outrage was way out of proportion.

"If *I* don't find it tasteless, I don't know why anyone would," he told the press. He would have said the same to a friend or a stranger on the street, and he managed to do exactly what I couldn't: stand up for himself without being defensive and unemotionally evaluate the true nature of the situation.

Drew was the cap to a crazy first year at *George* that was filled with constant change and conflicting demands. Everybody was riding high from the first issue, which flew off newsstands. The media faithfully talked about our magazine and kept the ride going. *George*'s notoriety grew to the point where it became difficult to concentrate on actually putting out a magazine. All the attention was a lot to manage for the editors, for me, and especially for John. He was an editor in chief who was so much more than that. His outside obligations were an added obstacle to meeting deadlines and the everyday business of publishing.

On top of all that, John was about to make another huge life change. He and Carolyn decided to get married that same September on Cumberland Island in Georgia.

By far the hardest part of the wedding process was keeping everything under wraps—that's what kept me up at night. For example, we couldn't send their wedding program to a printer because the risk of someone leaking the information was too high. So one night, Carolyn came to the office after hours to print her wedding programs on a copier that was far from professional grade. After a couple of mishaps involving the heavy card stock getting stuck in various maddening spots, we had to feed the printer one excruciating page at a time.

We finally finished with the programs at 11:30 p.m. Although I hadn't eaten since three in the afternoon, I was so tired I just wanted my bed. But once I got under the covers, panic set in because I couldn't remember if I had double-checked the printer for overlooked programs. I could just picture a *George* editor or someone from another magazine moseying down the hallway and seeing a piece of paper in the printer, reading it, and getting the biggest scoop of the year. And it would be my fault.

The most important aspect of this wedding for John and Carolyn was that it be private.

Fueled by the adrenaline that comes with fear, I threw on some clothes, ran downstairs, and flagged the sole cab driving up Third Avenue at the desolate hour of 1:30 a.m. I took the taxi back uptown to the office, my heart pounding for the entire ride. I tore out of the cab, into the building, and past security, who knew me well because I'd been to the office so often after hours. I ran directly to the copier, looked in, and to my great relief, found absolutely nothing. To put my mind fully at ease, I checked with the guard that nobody had come in after Carolyn and I left. I went home, got back in bed, and woke up after only a few hours of sleep, right back on high alert.

As John's assistant, I already had a long list of things that gave me insomnia: the next *George* cover getting leaked; my having to track down someone John wanted to interview for an upcoming issue; the person who would be mad at me that week for having to say, "No, I'm sorry. John can't do that." But during the lead-up to the wedding, I lived in a constant state of fear that I would somehow let the news slip.

I never told anybody about their plans—not my parents, not Matt, not Michele, or even Frank, with whom I shared absolutely everything. This news was too big. After Carolyn and John settled on a location and date, I didn't even let myself think about it too often. I didn't want that information front and center in my brain, ready to come out at the wrong time to the wrong person.

Since a big part of my job was dealing with the media, I tried to imagine what their marrying would mean to the outside world. My perspective on the situation was skewed, because John and Carolyn were so familiar to me. My instinct, when I thought about them getting married, was to wonder about normal stuff, such as whether they would stay in the same apartment or what her dress would look like. Not how their wedding would play out in the press. I just couldn't predict the impact of the news.

Certainly people—reporters, friends, media types—wanted to know if they were getting married. I was frequently asked that question. In the last couple of years of working for John, I mastered the art of being evasive. "Well, I think. Eventually," I'd say. "But who knows?"

I had learned such nonchalant ambiguity—not the same as lying—from John, the master of putting people off without hurt feelings or aroused suspicions. He used that strategy often with the press, who refused to stay on point when they had a chance to ask him questions. The most frequent question (besides whether he was going to get married) was whether he planned to run for office. "I'm really happy here [at *George*]," he told *USA Today*. "I'm serving a larger purpose in bringing more people to learn about politics. . . . My horizons are clear for the next five years, and after that, I'll sort of think about what the next horizon will be."

When it came to the media, John never got rattled, not even when he went on *Oprah* to publicize *George* shortly after the magazine's launch.

Sitting in the studio audience in Chicago during his appearance, I was nervous for John. Ironically, although he grew up in front of cameras, he'd never done national television, except for small segments on morning shows such as *Today* to publicize specific causes. But his being on *Oprah* was a big deal. In her introduction of him, Oprah used the word *hunk. He's going to hate that,* I thought.

John came out wearing a dark suit and the audience went insane. The women jumped out of their seats and screamed as if the Beatles were about to perform. He waved to the audience and they went even crazier. "John, we got new chairs for you," Oprah said, gushing like everyone else. *Gross,* I thought. John gave the talk-show host the same little bow that he politely offered any woman he met. His manners were always impeccable, whether he was at an employee's birthday party or on national TV.

Despite Oprah's adoration, she went down the track well worn by every other member of the media. After flashing a huge shot of him on-screen, coming out of the water in Hyannis, she asked how he'd respond to the charge of being an exhibitionist considering how often he was photographed shirtless.

"Not many people swim with their shirts on," he answered.

The studio audience swooned.

"How do you feel when people call you a hunk?"

"There are worse things people can say about you."

Women giggled.

"Who intimidates you?"

"Well, you do right now."

Applause.

Just like he did at the *George* press conference, he answered every question, but on his terms. He was smart about it and created humor in his evasion of the questions. Although John was an editor in chief, the most valuable PR lessons I learned were from him, ones I still use today.

John never did press without a clear idea of why he was doing it. He didn't go on *Larry King Live* or *Oprah* to do an interview; he went on to talk about *George* or his current cause. But he understood that the personal questions were in service of that mission, which helped him keep any aggravation in perspective. In the same vein, he never copped an attitude once he had agreed to an interview. He never gave Oprah or anyone else a list of questions not to ask him. If you don't want to be asked questions, then don't go on *Oprah,* he reasoned.

John knew you had to give a little to get a little when it came to publicity, and he kept his expectations realistic. But perhaps the most important aspect to his success with the media was that John wasn't afraid of being caught off guard. "Nothing is as good or bad as it seems in the moment," he told me. His example gave me perspective that I didn't always have because of my own emotional nature. By watching John, I became more levelheaded in my reactions and, as a result, was better able to deal with a wide range of situations. It was one of the best lessons he ever taught me.

After Oprah interviewed John that afternoon and they left the stage, I was sitting in the studio audience with *George*'s executive editor, Biz Mitchell, when Oprah reappeared and said, "Is there a RoseMarie Terenzio and Biz Mitchell in the audience? John would like to see you." We raised our hands, but so did every other woman in the room.

Escorted by a battalion of assistants, Biz and I made our way to the green room, which was decorated with old-fashioned barber chairs. "This place is great," I said to one of Oprah's army. "I know, isn't it?" the young woman said. "It's all Oprah's vision." "Yes," another interjected. "She picked out *everything*. Doesn't she have the best taste?" The women's enthusiasm made me wonder how much Kool-Aid they'd had that day or if the green room was bugged.

John walked in, looking tired but happy.

"You did really well," I said.

"That's nice of you to say."

John always said that when he was embarrassed (such as in the rare moments I complimented him on his suit or tie). He hated to talk about his TV appearances after the fact. Once they were done, so was he.

When Oprah walked into the green room, her acolytes smiled and stood up straighter. Even John seemed shocked by the sycophancy.

John introduced us. "This is RoseMarie," he said. Oprah shook my hand and replied, "You must be the helper."

"Nice to meet you," I said with all the energy of a moody teenager.

Oprah was unfazed, but her staffers were clearly having heart attacks. They all gave me dirty looks, but I knew John got a kick out of my bad attitude. I didn't treat Oprah any differently than I treated John. Still, he gave me shit about it in the parking lot.

"Nice, Rosie, way to step off on Oprah."

"Oh, shut up."

He laughed. "Do you think any of Oprah's people tell her to shut up?"

"No, but they should."

In the weeks leading up to John and Carolyn's wedding, the lessons I learned from John came in handy. I was really tense from pretending everything was business as usual at the magazine while coordinating the details of a top-secret event. To keep it together, I told myself that this was just two people getting married (adopting John's no-drama attitude), even though the question of their relationship status often made headlines.

That's why I thanked God when a rumor that John and Carolyn had broken up began circulating right before the big day. It was perfect. The speculation was based on their not being spotted out together for a couple of weeks—ironically, a function of being busy with the wedding preparations. I laughed out loud at an item that said Carolyn had been seen in a Paris café, sharing a romantic moment with a new mystery man. Her date turned out to be her good friend the designer Narciso Rodriguez, whom she'd met overseas for a wedding gown fitting.

Despite the moment of relief the news of their breakup afforded me, I quickly returned to being a nervous wreck. I was working late every night at the magazine, trying to get John to sign off on a million decisions before he left for three weeks for the wedding and honeymoon. Understandably, John was very distracted, which made my task that much harder.

As far as I knew, the rest of the magazine staff didn't have a clue about the wedding. They knew he was leaving for a trip but thought it was a kayaking vacation in Turkey. So I had to watch what I said around the office, which wasn't a problem except when I was talking on the phone to the innkeepers on Cumberland Island.

To keep the true subject of our conversations secret, we referred to the event as Nicole Miller's wedding. Why I would be talking about Nicole Miller's wedding doesn't make much sense now, and I'm sure if anyone at *George* paid attention to my phone conversations, they would have thought I was insane— or moonlighting as a wedding planner. As long as the *George* staff was kept in the dark about the real wedding, though, I didn't care what they thought.

By the time I watched Carolyn finish packing for her trip to Georgia, I didn't know who was more anxious, her or me. We went over and over the details as she placed perfectly folded shirts and accessories divided into ziplock bags into her suitcase. With every possible emergency anticipated and prepared for, she zipped up her bags and we headed downstairs, where a car waited to take her to the airport. The driver popped the trunk, threw her suitcases in, and opened the door for Carolyn, who looked elegant in a pair of brown corduroys, a black turtleneck, and black flats. Before getting inside, she turned to me, looking sad and concerned.

"I feel really bad, like I'm leaving you behind," Carolyn said.

She and I had discussed my attending the wedding, but I had decided not to go. If I were in Georgia, it would be obvious that something was up. As much as I would have liked to go as her and John's friend, I needed to stay in New York as their assistant, in case anything went wrong.

"I really appreciate that, but don't worry about it," I said to Carolyn before she got in the car. "I don't want to go."

"I don't blame you."

"That came out the wrong way," I added quickly.

"What if the wine doesn't show?"

"It'll show," I reassured her.

Once I saw her off to the airport, I returned home and made a call about the wine. Better safe than sorry.

While I was confirming the last of the travel arrangements, I thought about how the guest list was impossibly small. Only forty of their closest friends and family members were invited. For most people, that would be a tough number to stick to, but for them, it was ridiculous.

A lot of folks were going to be upset after the news broke. Being snubbed would be a big deal to them. Not going was a big deal to *me*—even though I was the one who'd decided it was for the best. Still, I was supposed to be in the couple's inner circle. And the thought of those who already doubted my position saying "How close to them could Rose be if she wasn't at their wedding?" really bugged me.

The truth is, I didn't want to go because the wedding was so small that some of their closest friends weren't invited. I worked for them, so it would have pissed a lot of people off—and I had enough of that in my job.

Once John and Carolyn left for Georgia, I went from being on edge to being completely paranoid. I felt as if the whole success—or failure—of the mission was on my shoulders. Of course, that wasn't true. The intricate plan that Carolyn had begun five months prior was in place, and my sole responsibility now was to tie up loose ends and keep my mouth shut. Still, it was a burden that at times felt too big.

At the office, when someone casually tossed off a question such as "Where's John going again?" I became suspicious. *They're fishing,* I thought. *They know.* I also took my anxiety out on my friends—particularly Michele and Frank. The people you feel closest to always get the brunt of it, because you know you can get away with it. No matter how lousy I acted toward Michele and Frank, I knew they'd still love me the next day. But I'll admit, I did test their limits.

The Thursday before the wedding, I had made a plan to meet Michele after work and wound up leaving her sitting by herself in a bar for over an hour. When I finally walked in, instead of apologizing, I acted like I was the one who'd been inconvenienced. Having spent the last couple of hours trying to coordinate plane reservations and ferry trips for guests, I was wound tight.

"You couldn't possibly understand how stressful my life is," I said to Michele.

"You're right. I can't, because you don't tell me what's going on," she said.

Faced with her genuine concern, I realized how inconsiderate I'd been and decided to make a radical departure from my paranoid self. I told Michele the secret.

Immediately, I felt unburdened. In an instant, she recognized the strain I'd been under for the last few weeks and offered me the comfort I'd been craving. I didn't worry, either, because I knew Michele wouldn't breathe the news. In fact, the next day, she called me very early in the morning because she hadn't been able to sleep.

"Now that I know, I'm nervous, too," she said.

The only person to whom I didn't betray any sign of nerves was Carolyn. She and I talked about fifteen million times in between her arriving on Cumberland Island and the wedding. Her questions were breezy enough—discussing the reservations and coordinating times for the guests' departures—and my answers were reassuring: everything was under control and would turn out fine.

By late afternoon on the Friday before the ceremony, I started to loosen up. The press had yet to call me with questions about a wedding, so in my mind, we were in the clear. At that point, even if the media did get wind of John and Carolyn's plans, by the time the papers went to press (this was the pre-Internet era), the wedding already would have happened. Of course, television could still be a problem—but a security detail ensured only the guests were allowed on the private island.

That evening, while the guests on Cumberland Island were enjoying cocktails, I sat in my apartment unable to share the news with anyone. *I have to get out of here,* I thought. The four walls, the quiet, were getting to me. I decided to flee to my parents' house. I could check my voice mail easily enough from there, and I didn't need to sit by the phone anyway, since the statement and details of John and Carolyn's marriage were being released by Ted Kennedy's office (thankfully, they'd be dealing with the aftermath).

The next day, after eating a big lunch with my parents, I checked my voice mail for the hundredth time that day and heard a panicked message from Matt Berman and Biz Mitchell. I called them back immediately.

There was a problem: After Jack Nicholson agreed to appear as dirty Santa Claus (instead of Marlon Brando), with a cigarette hanging out of his mouth, on the cover of *George*'s holiday issue, a photo shoot was set for the Saturday of the wedding. But the actor never showed up to the studio, and the crew couldn't reach him or his assistant. Biz and Matt had resorted to driving around New York City, trying to find the set where Jack was filming his latest movie.

"We need John to call him," Matt said.

I cringed. "Sorry, he can't. He's totally unavailable."

"Can't you just call him? We aren't going to have a cover. This is an emergency."

They were panicked, and I felt horrible. But there was nothing I could do. I couldn't call John on his wedding day because of a problem with Jack Nicholson. John wouldn't have considered the situation an emergency.

"I can't reach him today," I said. "I don't know what to say. I'm really sorry, guys."

Biz and Matt never did find Jack Nicholson and, I'm sure, cursed me for refusing to call John (we wound up putting Woody Harrelson in angel wings on the cover). But they soon found out, along with the rest of the world, why John was unreachable on Saturday. The wedding went off without a hitch, and on Sunday—rather than the news of their marriage being announced in a formal press release to the AP as planned—Patrick Kennedy, who hadn't been invited to the wedding, blurted out at a Democratic fund-raiser, "My cousin John did tie the knot yesterday."

No sooner had the words come out of his mouth Sunday than my home phone lit up with incoming calls from all over the world. I received fifty-three voice mail messages in one hour. While I listened to the phone ring over and over, the bulk of the calls completely overloaded my answering machine and broke it. I called my contact in Teddy's office and informed her of the call volume; we laughed about Patrick's surprise press conference, and I wished her luck.

I went to the office on Monday around 7:00 a.m. to put a bottle of champagne on each female staffer's desk and cigars on the guys', along with a personal note from John stating the obvious—he'd gotten married—and thanking everyone for their hard work. "It's an honor to have you as colleagues," he wrote. "This magazine has turned the corner, and it ain't because Fauntleroy does Oprah."

After I had finished passing out the gifts, the private phone line (which only John, Carolyn, and a handful of other people knew the number of) rang at my desk: it was John and Carolyn.

"Oh my God, so what happened?" Carolyn said. "How's it going? Is it in the papers?"

"What? Are you kidding me? It's everywhere on the planet."

"Jesus."

"I can't wait to see all the photos. The dress looked amazing in the pictures I saw."

"Oh my God, the dress. I couldn't get it over my head at first. I was freaking out. But Gordon saved the day. He put a silk scarf over my head and eased the dress down that way."

"No fucking way."

John grabbed the phone. "Hey, stupid," he said.

"Hey, stupid, congrats," I replied. "How does it feel?"

"It's really great," John said happily.

"It means you're old, you know."

I was psyched they had called me. It was funny and sweet that the Monday morning after their wedding, they wanted to talk to me and make me feel included, even though I couldn't be there.

CHAPTER
8

The media had always covered John and Carolyn, but after they got married, the paparazzi were relentless. At first, it was all about the wedding. For weeks after, people were still hunting for information. So much so that when Frank and I went on vacation to Paris the week after their wedding, we were photographed sitting at a café with Narciso, whom we were visiting. The photo was published in *People* magazine. I understood the media were trying to find a story, but that was a stretch. When John and Carolyn returned from their honeymoon, photographers and reporters were camped outside the house every day, and their constant presence was stressful for the couple.

I also got a taste of the paparazzi's rabidity when John invited me to a Knicks game the January before they were married.

"What are you doing for your birthday on Tuesday night?" John asked me.

"Nothing. I'm celebrating on Friday and Saturday night."

"Do you want to go to the Knicks–Bulls game with me?"

"Oh, you don't have to take me, John. You can just give me the tickets and I can take a friend."

"You're such a bitch, Rosie. I want to go, too."

"No, no! I'm sorry. I didn't mean it like that. I just meant that if you would rather not go, you don't have to just because it's my birthday."

"I want to take you."

"Great! Thank you."

It was an unseasonably warm night, so John decided that he wanted to walk the fifteen blocks from the office to Madison Square Garden. He extended his arm for me to hold on to and said, "You're my date tonight, Rosie." It was fun to be out with him socially for a change. I didn't have letters to write or appointments to schedule, just the easy enjoyment of chatting about friends, the office, and life as we walked arm in arm, anonymous amid the crowds of midtown workers making their way to Penn Station.

We were halfway there when out of the blue, John said, "Rosie, why don't we grab a cab?"

I looked at him like he was crazy. "Why? I thought we were walking. We're only seven blocks away."

"Just get a cab."

I dropped his arm and stepped into the street to hail a taxi when the paparazzi descended like pigeons flying in to attack a half-eaten pretzel on the ground. I'd been totally oblivious to the signs, but with a practiced eye, John immediately saw them coming.

As soon as I raised my arm to flag down a cab, at least ten

of them appeared out of nowhere, screaming his name when they realized he was about to get away. *Flash, flash, flash!* Their cameras made my head spin. I almost fell on my ass in the traffic whizzing down Seventh Avenue. John allowed them to take a few pictures, and then maneuvered like a missile into the cab (head down, eyes up), as I tumbled in behind him.

Inside the cab, we waited at a red light, while the paparazzi snapped shot after shot, their flashes illuminating the car's interior. John looked out the window, oddly embarrassed that I had witnessed firsthand the craziness that accompanied him wherever he went. The cabdriver broke the awkward silence by telling John how best to avoid the paparazzi on his bike.

"Listen, man, if you want to lose the photographers, you have to ride *against* traffic."

"Thanks for the tip," John said, then turned to me, smiling, and said, "Somebody's life is going to be a freak show tomorrow."

"What are you talking about?" I asked.

"You'll see."

Two days later, the *Daily News* ran a picture of my big date with John. Not to be outdone on the JFK Jr. beat, the other tabloids quickly followed with their own items and photos of the night. The *New York Post* published a story identifying me by name. The *Globe* ran with the cover headline "JFK Jr.'s Hot Date with his Secretary," and inside the paper: "By George, JFK Jr. Puts in Overtime." Meanwhile, I couldn't have been happier, because the article called me a "twenty-five-year-old beauty."

"Every word of it is true," I joked to my friends about the piece.

But of course it wasn't, particularly the part about my

knowing "never to order cream of broccoli soup for John's lunch—because he hates it." John, the least picky eater I'd ever met, consumed whatever I got for him and half of my lunch every day. He would have dined on ground cardboard if I put enough salt and pepper on it.

When the press about our "hot date" hit, John seized the opportunity to mock me, poking fun at my coat in one picture by calling it "roadkill." He wasn't the only one who enjoyed my fifteen minutes of fame. My family, Frank's family, and all my friends loved the article. My mother bought every single copy of the *Globe* at her local supermarket.

"Mom, there's a lot of stuff in there that's completely made up," I said.

"You work for him and went to the game. That's enough truth for me."

John lost his cool with the paparazzi only a handful of times. One involved a contentious issue—his dog. You could yell at John, call him a pretty boy, or even call him dumb, but you didn't mess with Friday, the Canaan puppy he brought home a few months before getting married. Usually as affable with the paparazzi as he was with everyone else, John was less than charitable when he witnessed, through the picture window of the restaurant where he was eating breakfast with Carolyn, a particularly crazy paparazzo named Ruth untying Friday, picking him up, and putting him on her lap to pet him. The provocation worked. John tore out of the restaurant, yanked the leash away, and snarled, "Don't you *ever* touch my dog." Other than taking photos, that's what the paparazzi do: they try to get a rise out of you. And Ruth was brilliant at it. Despite her matted hair and oversized, frayed T-shirts, the fifty-something-year-old had a knack for getting into highly secure places, such as private parties—and the *George* offices. Once, an editor reported that a strange, unfamiliar woman was using the copy machine. I went over to find out what was up.

"Ruth!" I yelled at the sight of the crumpled little woman, weighed down by her camera bags and hovering over the copier. "Get out of here."

"I'm just copying something," she said.

"It's illegal for you to be in here."

"I'll be done in a sec."

I felt sorry for her and often let her take a couple of pictures at an event before ushering her out, knowing full well that she'd be back if she could find a way. But by sneaking into the office, she had gone too far.

Another incident with the paparazzi happened after John called me from Hyannis one summer weekend to let me know we had a problem. It turned out that "our" problem stemmed from John having dumped a bucket of water over the head of a photographer who wouldn't stop taking pictures of Carolyn on the beach every time John went into the water and wasn't there to protect her. Regretting his reaction a few moments later, John left a note on the photographer's car with the office address and the message that he would pay for the damaged camera. He also spelled the word *address* incorrectly.

Of course, the photographer fed the misspelled note to a newspaper and sent us a fifteen-thousand-dollar bill for the damaged camera. What was the camera made of—gold? Asking for repayment for the broken camera was one thing; quadrupling the price just because it was John Kennedy who'd damaged it was quite another. I wasn't going to let that happen; I called the photographer to tell him that now John wouldn't be sending any money.

When John wasn't by Carolyn's side, the photographers released the full force of their aggression, which, needless to say, was pretty aggressive. Whenever she went out—to get a coffee, walk the dog, or meet a friend—they were there, pushing in close and shouting things like "whore" and "bitch." And worse.

I was shocked at the display of raw meanness but understood why they resorted to nasty name-calling. Always discreet and reserved in public, Carolyn gave them nothing.

Carolyn couldn't simply pose and then move on like John did, and anyway, it wasn't that easy. Those staid pictures weren't sellable: a paparazzo makes more money off a shot if there's some action or emotion in it. If they could break her perfect exterior, it would be an instant story: "Carolyn on Verge of Nervous Breakdown" or "Problems at Home for Newlyweds." So they reached new levels of viciousness and patiently waited for her to mess up, act out, or go crazy. I tried to cheer her up with a joke when she'd call, upset. "I don't know why you said yes to John. I would have said no." But I pitied her; the girl was basically a sitting duck.

"This is ridiculous," she said, calling me at the office one day. "If I don't leave the house before 8:00 a.m., they're waiting for me. *Every* morning."

I didn't know what to say.

"They chase me down the street," Carolyn continued.

"Just try to smile and don't say a fucking word," I told her.

I always stressed to Carolyn that she shouldn't let the press, the paparazzi, or cameramen hear her voice. A person's voice is personal and intimate. If they never heard hers, I thought, they wouldn't get what they wanted.

After two weeks of constant post-wedding madness, even John, despite his usual "suck it up" attitude, was at his breaking point. The number of paparazzi outside their apartment building had tripled and didn't show any signs of abating.

"Rose, I'm going to confront them," John said over the phone from their apartment. "This is out of hand. I'm going downstairs to give a statement, and then Carolyn and I will take a few pictures."

Making an in-person statement to the press was revolutionary for a guy who never, ever addressed his personal life in public.

"What are you going to say?" I asked.

"I'll say that we're flattered by the attention, but that Carolyn needs a break. She's not as used to this as I am."

He was going to try to charm them.

Carolyn had her doubts. She grabbed the phone.

"I don't want to go down there," she said. "I'm not sure this is a good idea."

"They just want a shot of you two together, the newlyweds. And then they have it. I think it's a good idea. You don't have to say anything, or even smile. Just stand there."

Soon after we got off the phone, Carolyn, dressed in a long, elegant camel-colored skirt, stood holding her new husband's hand on the steps of their building while John gave a speech to the photographers, who were snapping away.

If the paparazzi got some good shots and took John's plea to heart, I thought they would go away and let John and Carolyn enjoy their life. That's what we were all hoping for, but the odds weren't good.

While Carolyn was dealing with the unwavering attention on her marriage, I was dealing with the scrutiny on a professional level, and it definitely made my job harder. Although we were coming at it from different angles, we were in the same boat. With both of us trying to keep it together and scared about somehow messing up, we commiserated many times a day by phone.

The toughest part for me was keeping the focus on *George* amid all the nuttiness. John had done well positioning himself as an editor in chief and tried to let his magazine, rather than him, become the object of interest. I refused to let all that hard work go to waste.

Even internally, their new marriage changed things. Now that John had made his relationship with Carolyn official, some people at Hachette acted as if she were also the official property of the magazine. She wasn't part of the equation before, but now some of the execs wanted to trot her out in the same dog-and-pony show they pressured John to be a part of.

The publishing company's top brass had always tried to exploit John's celebrity in ways that didn't necessarily benefit *George*. While it was part of John's job description to woo advertisers, Hachette's CEO David Pecker seemed to find any excuse to make John go to dinner with clients.

When Pecker's requests first starting rolling in, I'd politely take the calls from his assistant and relay the requests to John, who would invariably say yes. But soon his calendar was almost completely filled up by dinners with would-be advertisers. Despite endless dining experiences with CEOs, fashion designers, and media planners, John couldn't get those companies to advertise enough, if at all, in *George*'s pages. Pecker seemed to be pulling a shell game—entertaining them with John's presence while encouraging them to spend their money on more appealing Hachette titles.

After the initial frenzy of *George*'s launch, the ad sales plummeted a few issues in and the magazine grew noticeably thinner. Pecker in turn became more brazen in his requirements of John, putting constant pressure on him to drum up business.

After the requests became twice-a-week affairs, or more, I went into John's office for a reality check.

"You know, it's really interesting that *Elle* has thirteen pages of Liz Claiborne ads and we have two. How many times has *Elle*'s editor in chief gone to dinner with their people?"

"All right, Rosie. Let's just calm down."

"You've got to start saying no to this bullshit."

He tried going up to Pecker's office, but Pecker talked him out of his objections. I didn't blame John for being cowed by Pecker. *George*'s contract with Hachette was up at the end of the following year, and the magazine still hadn't turned a profit. That was not unusual for a magazine but it was unacceptable for one with John as editor in chief, so Pecker had the upper hand.

John worked so hard, putting everything he had into that magazine, and Hachette was not backing *George* with the sorely needed marketing and advertising muscle. John had to be a diplomat, but I didn't. It was my job to manage John's time, and many of Pecker's dinner requests weren't a good use of it. (Though Pecker didn't quite see my role the same way.) So I started refusing them.

"No, he's not meeting with Seagram's again."

"No, he's not going to dinner with the Mercedes-Benz people for a third time."

The subtext being: *No, he's not Pecker's puppet.*

Soon after I had wrestled John's schedule from Pecker's grip, he called John to complain. "I signed a contract to work with John Kennedy," he said, seething. "Not RoseMarie Terenzio."

Many people shared that sentiment—including some on the *George* staff—because I didn't think twice about stepping in when I saw him compromising himself for the magazine, which he came very close to doing during the Monica Lewinsky scandal.

I sensed something was up when John came out of an editorial planning meeting on the magazine's coverage of President Clinton's extramarital affair with the White House intern. He brushed me off when I asked what had been discussed. John and Carolyn both tried to avoid me when they knew I was skeptical of something, which made me feel like a hall monitor.

Later, John asked me to type up a letter from his notes. As soon as I made sense of what I was writing, I stopped and stormed into his office. The letter personally requested an interview with Monica Lewinsky. I understood that controversy sold magazines, and I certainly didn't think John needed to be cautious journalistically. I had no problem when he wanted to push the envelope with the Marilyn Monroe cover (or even with the idea of dressing Madonna as his mom), but this was going too far.

"There is no way you are interviewing Monica Lewinsky," I yelled.

"You don't get it, Rose," he said, turning his back to me.

"I get it. I get that you're going to find someone else on the staff to do it."

"I'm the only one who can land this."

It would have been great for the magazine, but terrible for John. We had a hard enough time getting people to take him seriously. As far as I was concerned, interviewing Monica Lewinsky was low-hanging fruit for John Kennedy. "You don't need to sell magazines that badly, and she's not a political figure," I said.

"Yes, she is. She's in the middle of the biggest political scandal in recent history."

"I respectfully disagree with you on this one. And this isn't something you'll be comfortable with once it's done. You'll regret it."

"Every reputable magazine is trying to get this."

"Okay, let me spell it out for you. If you get the interview, everyone will say it's just because of who you are. And then they'll rehash the rumors about your father in the White House." And I knew I would be the one cleaning up the mess, propping him up through his regret while I fended off a million calls from the press. I ended up winning the fight. For *George*'s Sex in High Places issue, John settled on a tamer historical perspective by interviewing Gary Hart—an actual political figure whose career in the Senate ended in the eighties after his extramarital affair was exposed.

The day after our argument, I came into work to find on my desk a big cardboard box. On its side was a drawing of a girl with a speech bubble containing the word "No!"

"I don't think I need you anymore," John said, pointing at my replacement. "I have her."

I was gaining more confidence at *George,* and not just in saying no to John. I started to have an editorial influence, helping to brainstorm cover ideas or suggesting interview subjects for John. I even interviewed the Democratic strategist James Carville for the magazine's back-page "If I Were President" feature. Among the editors, I now had allies and friends. In addition to Matt Berman and Biz, the executive editor, others learned I had more to contribute than just my gatekeeper duties (even the editor who had mocked me about PBS was in my corner). I began to feel as if I belonged, and I realized over drinks, during late closes, and even at parties that they didn't see me as the dumb girl from the Bronx that I thought they had. While I continued to butt heads with some editors who didn't consider me to be anything more than in their way, most of them came to understand that my saying no to John and looking out for him was an asset rather than a hindrance. At the end of the day, my concern was always for John over the magazine.

And the same was true for Carolyn. After they were married, I had to start saying no for her, too. Once their relationship became official, she had more responsibilities, as she knew she would. She had to consider both John's social obligations and his responsibilities to the magazine. For example, when attending a public event, she wouldn't wear any designer that advertised in *George* for fear of angering other designers who might pull their ad pages. Because designers came out of the woodwork wanting to dress her, I had to turn down quite a few offers.

Getting Carolyn to wear a designer's dress or carry their handbag was a surefire way to sell clothes and, as some of the sales reps at *George* soon realized, also a great way to sell ads. The sales reps started pushing for Carolyn to join John for dinners with designers, asking that she wear certain clothes. That's when I began taking a more aggressive approach in turning people down.

One ad sales rep cornered me while I was in the ladies' room and told me that an important client wanted John and Carolyn to come to his apartment and have breakfast with him, his wife, and his kids.

"A monkey could sell those ad pages by getting John Kennedy and his wife to come for breakfast," I said, thinking, *And if we had a monkey, then we wouldn't need you.* Basing sales on John's meeting with clients was a supremely flawed concept. After you sell the first set of ads based on meeting John, how do you top that?

"What do we do to get him to buy pages next year?" I asked. "Let him sleep with Carolyn?"

The sales rep, who stormed out of the bathroom, made the mistake of approaching John about the breakfast. His response was a firm, terse no. Whenever anyone went to John in an attempt to get a different answer from the one I had offered, they were usually disappointed. At that point, John and I were on the same page about almost everything. He appreciated the role I took in protecting Carolyn in addition to him, because he wasn't always in a position to do that. And I was now fully confident in my ability to determine what was a yes and what was a no.

While protecting John and Carolyn was getting easier, protecting Frank, something I had done throughout our relationship, had just become more difficult. No matter what he asked for or what time of night he needed me to meet him, I was always there. When Frank didn't write a final paper for a class, I wrote it for him. Before I found him a job, I paid his bills for six months because he had no money. And when he tested positive for HIV, I was the only one he told.

When Frank mentioned that he was getting tested, I didn't think much of it. He had assured me he was always safe (plus, I didn't believe that anything harmful could ever befall Frank). It took two weeks to get the results, so when he called me at work with the news, it seemed out of the blue. And totally terrifying. We spent several months in denial, until we told my sister Amy, a nurse practitioner, who got Frank in to see a top AIDS specialist. The doctor, who saw Frank for free because of her relationship with my sister, prescribed a drug cocktail.

The regimen of drugs to manage HIV was grueling. He had to take roughly ten pills a day, some with food, some on an empty stomach, and some in the middle of the night. Routine wasn't Frank's forte, and the drug schedule was something he needed to stick to religiously to stay alive. I was so scared he would miss a dose that I called him at 3:00 a.m. every day to make sure he took his pill.

As close as we were, Frank and I found ourselves at odds because of our jobs, a particularly painful experience. Frank's boss, Brad Johns, Carolyn's colorist, often talked about her to the media. After the wedding, he was in the paper every other day, giving tons of elaborate details about her hair and how he'd colored it before the wedding ceremony. Carolyn and John were pissed that Brad wouldn't shut his mouth and threatened to take legal action in a cease-and-desist letter.

John, who tried to avoid lawsuits, asked me to appeal to Frank, who might be able to stop Brad's loquaciousness. John thought a simple threat would put an end to the nonsense. But to me there was nothing simple about that call. I felt sick to my stomach dialing Frank's number. In the million times I had called him, we'd never been on opposite sides.

Once I'd relayed John and Carolyn's complaint, he said, "There's nothing I can do. I have to do what he tells me to."

Following a quiet moment of tension, I fell into my old habit of getting angry when uncomfortable. "You're making my job and my life miserable. Your loyalty is supposed to be to me," I said.

"I don't know what to do," he said, on the verge of tears.

"Then I have to send him a cease-and-desist letter."

"Okay, I'll make sure Brad gets it," he said.

I felt as if I had failed John by not immediately solving the problem, and failed Frank by not being able to protect him.

As promised, I sent the letter, and sure enough, the items stopped appearing in the papers. For John and Carolyn the issue was resolved. But for Frank, his problems had just begun. Not long after he got the letter, he was fired. Frank was heartbroken; for the first time, he'd felt as if he was starting a career. Working for the salon changed him. He had begun getting up early in the morning and going to the gym before work.

As soon as he was let go, Frank went back to his old habits—drinking heavily, staying out until all hours of the night, experimenting with God knows who or what. I wasn't going to let his getting fired by a hair salon derail him, so I set about finding him another job. Negi Vafa, *George*'s creative services director, a chic Iranian woman, hired Frank to assist her with RSVPs and to man the door at events.

Even John pitched in to the effort to keep Frank gainfully employed by paying him to drive his Buckeye Powered Parachute—a contraption that looked like a flying lawn mower—to the Midwest to be fixed. John, traveling for the magazine, met Frank in Chicago to give the renewed Buckeye a test drive; that way, if any problems occurred, Frank could drive it back to the shop for further repairs. When they checked in to a Holiday Inn, the receptionist looked at JFK Jr., standing next to an equally, if not more, handsome man, and asked nervously, "Who's the nonsmoking queen?"

Frank waved his hand theatrically and said, "That would be me."

John loved that story—he got a ton of mileage out of recounting their buddy-comedy road trip. Of course, Frank charmed everyone: grouchy middle-aged diner waitresses, bitchy queens, even movie stars. I once brought him as my date to a dinner at the apartment of John's sister, Caroline. She hosted an evening for friends and family to celebrate John and Carolyn's marriage. Julia Roberts, who was dating John's trainer, sat at our table, and of course Frank had her wrapped around his finger before the salad plates were cleared. When he got up to go to the bathroom, Julia leaned toward me and whispered, "I hope you're going to marry him. He's a great guy and he's so gorgeous."

"I know, Julia," I replied, "but he's gay."

"Are you sure?" she said, looking disappointed.

I could take Frank anywhere, and he would not only hold his own but become part of the scene. He was even in a newspaper's coverage of the dinner. The paparazzi snapped Frank helping Carolyn carry her gifts as they exited Caroline's building, and the photo appeared in the paper the next day. Not Julia Roberts. Not Caroline Kennedy. Frank Giordano.

Frank definitely was the life of the party, which wasn't always a good thing—especially for him. He'd often repeat his signature line, "I know, I know, I have to get off the party carousel," but still found a reason to go out almost every night of the week. And everyone knew he was the one with access to the "party favors."

From my point of view, Frank's problems with alcohol and drugs—as with his inability to secure long-term employment— were just a by-product of Frank being Frank. I never considered that he was an addict; instead I naively believed he just needed to grow up. The hardest drug I ever did was pot, so I decided the alarm I felt in regard to Frank's excessive drug use was simply an overreaction. I assumed that Frank's HIV diagnosis would be a wake-up call, but Frank just kept partying. To protect myself from the truth, I turned his drug use into another item on the list of Frank's selfish acts. There was always drama where Frank was concerned. He refused to grow up and I was getting sick of taking care of him. After all the lost jobs, car accidents, and failed relationships he'd been through, I was tired of worrying.

His carelessness wasn't mean-spirited or intentional, but his substance abuse was taking over his life. So I should have known it was a mistake to put Frank in charge of the main dish at a birthday dinner I threw for myself. It was 1997, and Matt Berman had offered to host a dinner party for me at his new apartment, a gorgeous loft in SoHo that he had decorated to perfection (you found yourself wanting everything in that apartment, whether it was a fifty-dollar lamp or a thousand-dollar photograph).

I planned a glamorous dinner party and decided to cook for ten of my best friends against the backdrop of the lights of Manhattan filtering through the apartment's huge windows. Frank, who wanted to help and do something nice for me, had insisted on buying the leg of lamb for the main course. He was supposed to arrive at Matt's at 5:00 p.m. so I'd have enough time to cook the meat, but he didn't show up until 6:30 p.m., when the first guests began trickling in for cocktail hour. I was livid but decided not to say anything, so as not to make a scene in front of the other guests.

"Here you go, Ro," he said, thrusting a big bag into my arms. "Happy birthday!"

He looked a little off, but I just took the package into the kitchen and began to unwrap it—only to discover it was not lamb but a supermarket-prepared pork roast that would feed about four people. I wanted to cry. I walked right up to Frank, who was pouring wine into a water glass, and got in his face.

"It's not funny anymore, Frank," I said. "It's my birthday, I asked you to do one thing, and you can't get it right, after everything I've done for you?"

Frank looked at me as if he didn't have a care in the world. "I never asked you to do any of that for me," he said matter-of-factly.

I was crushed; I felt as if Frank was telling me to go fuck myself for caring about him. We had been each other's favorite person for so long. But maybe that wasn't such a good thing. Frank was living his life as a gay guy with me as his best friend. I was living mine like a straight girl with a boyfriend who happened to be gay. I was so consumed with taking care of him that I didn't pay enough attention to other guys. Who could blame me? Frank and I were completely compatible, everyone loved him, and he was always up for anything. It was easier to be around Frank than most guys. Until now.

I had often put Frank's needs before mine with the understanding that we cared about each other. But the sleepless nights of worry, the incessant eye to detail, the obsession with loyalty—all of that was apparently *my* problem.

CHAPTER
9
———

Hachette had begun putting intense pressure on the staff to improve *George*'s numbers. Their threat to pull the plug if we didn't increase revenue became more real every day. As a result, I didn't have much time to focus on Frank and his problems. I saved all my worrying for the magazine, and so did John.

In November 1997, John rented the Beaverkill Valley Inn in the Catskills for an editorial retreat with the entire staff. The aim was to get everyone invested in the success of the magazine. After all, what's better for boosting morale than a rustic lodge in upstate New York during one of the dreariest months of the year?

We got the full camp experience, with meals served family-style around a big table (preceded by the requisite jockeying to sit next to everyone's favorite camp counselor and editor in chief). We went on hikes, which entailed pasty-faced city slickers in unsuitable footwear stumbling over rocks and roots, and of course we played soccer, with John trying not to embarrass his winded editors.

In between the nature walks and canteen meals, John held meeting after meeting to get everyone up to speed on what he hoped would be an aggressive and profitable new year. On the last day of the retreat, we gathered in one of the lodge's conference rooms to talk about newsstand competition. Sitting around tables set up in a U-shaped arrangement, we listened to the rain beat down on the paned-glass ceiling as John laid out his strategy to beat magazines such as *Men's Journal* and *Esquire,* amid cheerful rejoinders from the editors.

Finally, I couldn't help but point out the eight-hundred-pound gorilla in the room.

"We have half the staff of those other magazines," I said. "It's never going to happen unless Hachette steps up and gives us what we need to be competitive."

John glowered at me, gripping his pen a little too tightly.

"That's enough," he said in an unusually harsh tone.

"But—"

"I said that's *enough*! We don't need to hear that anymore."

His words were like a slap across my face. I turned beet red, humiliated in front of the editors, who quickly averted their gazes. I felt as if I were a teenager getting screamed at by my dad in front of my friends. After the initial sting of his rebuke wore off, a numbing rage took hold, and I shut out John and the rest of the room. Those people had become my colleagues and friends, and in one sentence he had made me feel like an idiot again.

When the meeting was over, everyone avoided me like the plague. They were visibly uncomfortable after witnessing John lash out at me—it had shocked them almost as much as it had embarrassed me. They weren't used to it. But I was. When he had a lot going on at once and felt overwhelmed, John would snap at me—something he didn't do with other people. I'd be filling out his expense reports and he'd irrationally bark, "Do you think that's a good use of your time?" I could tick off a laundry list of things I'd done for him that day—set up a week's worth of meetings, gather story ideas from all the editors, turn down invitations to events, follow up on a cover entreaty, draft a letter for his next interview request, drop off his prescription at the pharmacy, pick up a gift for a friend—and if he was in a bad mood, his response would be to look at me as if I were a moron and ask, "What about the brakes on my bike that need to be fixed?"

For all the benefits, interesting moments, and glamour that came with my proximity to and close relationship with John, there was also a downside that left me feeling utterly powerless. I was like family to him, and because he felt so comfortable with me, he also took me for granted and acted out his stress on me.

It was particularly awful when others witnessed it. The daughter of Nancy Haberman—a high-powered publicist at Rubenstein Associates, who handled press for the magazine— was an intern at *George,* answering my phone one afternoon, when she called out to John that someone was on the line for him. He yelled back in an extremely nasty tone, "What are you saying? I can't even hear you!" I heard *him* as I returned to my desk, where I found Nancy's daughter in total shock.

"John, that's not me. It's Maggie," I said.

"Oops," he said. "Sorry, Maggie."

Maggie later called her mother and said, "I can't believe how he talks to her sometimes."

When John was in a bad mood, Matt and I joked about it to ease the tension. Matt instantly would read my expression and ask if it was a "because I said so" or "opposite" day. He came up with the two categories as a joke based on a very real truth. On "because I said so" days, John fired off orders and then got on my case, as if expecting incompetence. "Did you send out that package?" he might ask five minutes after making the initial request. I knew better than to try to defend myself. On "opposite" days, I couldn't get anything right. Even if I did exactly what he told me to do, it was wrong. If I ordered Thai food for lunch after sussing out what he was in the mood for, he'd act completely shocked and unhappy with the choice. "Thai food? I had Thai food last night for dinner." At the end of either kind of day, I'd wind up in the bathroom, wringing myself out.

The difference between me and John, though, was that I never lashed out at him in public—and not only because he was my boss. For me, it was just like the scene in *The Godfather* when Michael Corleone tells Fredo to never take sides against the family. John's outburst at the staff retreat made me feel as if he didn't have my back. If he'd blasted the shit out of me after the meeting, that would have been fine. But to admonish me in front of a roomful of people crossed the line.

Back in my room, still seething, I was shoving clothes into my bag when John knocked on the door. I let him in, turned my back, and continued packing.

"I just spoke to Carolyn," he said. "She had no idea about the party tonight. Did you forget to tell her?"

I almost shredded the tank top in my hands. The magazine was holding a party that night to mark its second anniversary. Celebrities such as Sheryl Crow, Donald Trump, and Adam Duritz from Counting Crows had been invited to celebrate at the hot new restaurant Asia de Cuba. After the day I'd had, I would rather have put a stiletto through my hand than attend the event. Carolyn, who had known about it for weeks, was trying to get out of it by playing dumb, and I had no patience for it today.

"Boy, I'm getting it from all angles today. I can't get a break."

"Well, that's what she said," John replied.

"That's bullshit," I said, spinning around to face him. "Of course I told her. She just doesn't want to go."

John, suddenly uncomfortable, tried to change the subject.

"Look, I'm sorry about today's meeting. But when you say stuff like that, people assume it's coming from me. I can't go around being negative all the time about Hachette. It's bad for morale and bad for business."

Point taken. He'd just spent the whole weekend galvanizing the staff to do more with less, and I had to open my big mouth and rain on his parade. He was right to be annoyed. But I wasn't going to let him accuse me of not informing Carolyn about the party.

"Do you really think I'd forget to tell Carolyn about tonight? That's what sucks. After every little thing that I do for this place, you think I would forget that?"

He nodded and left me to finish packing, each of us understanding the other's position and agreeing to drop it. I had the unenviable task of running interference between John and Carolyn when they didn't feel like dealing with an issue. In moments like that—John needing Carolyn to attend the kind of public event she had come to dread and neither wanting to confront the other—I became a convenient pawn in their conversations, part assistant and part girl passing notes in class. It was the part of the job that neither of us wanted to examine too closely.

I didn't blame Carolyn for trying to skip the anniversary party (even if she did use me as the fall guy). The first year of marriage is hard for anyone; for her it was almost impossible. The meaner the stories in the press, the more Carolyn retreated into herself. The process was heartbreaking to witness and made me want to kill people who said, "Well, she knew what she was getting into when she married John." Just because someone knows what she's getting into doesn't make her life any easier. And how could Carolyn possibly have known the extent of it beforehand? I sure had no idea what I was getting into when I took the job with John.

After more than three years of working for him, I worried all the time. Every day, before the alarm clock went off, I woke up, popped out of bed, threw on some sweatpants and a T-shirt, and rushed to the Korean deli on the corner with my stomach in knots. I didn't wait to get back to my apartment to scan the papers for mentions of John, Carolyn, and *George*; I braced myself and looked through them on my walk home. After all those years, I still worried I would slip up and say the wrong thing. (Although that was the last thing I needed to be concerned about. As my friend Michele said, "The only way something you know could appear in the paper is if Page Six's editor slept inside your head, because you don't say anything to anybody.")

I wasn't just worried about a leak to the press. I was

concerned about everything—wondering how the latest issue had sold on newsstands and whether John and Carolyn should attend an event, making sure John's editor's letter was in on time and that every aspect of his life was in check. I couldn't let my guard down and just relax. And I certainly couldn't rely on John to put me at ease.

Unfortunately, John didn't understand why the paparazzi made Carolyn so upset or why I was so neurotic. "It's no big deal," he said to Carolyn over the phone in response to her complaining about a particularly vicious incident. "Just don't pay attention to it. I don't." I cringed. "There are worse things that could happen than a few photographers following you around," he said, putting the nail in the coffin of my afternoon; I now would have to clean up the mess he created by minimizing her feelings.

I knew that John's dismissive attitude was due to his frustration. He had no control over the situation and was angry that he couldn't protect his wife from it. He should have told her as much—I know she really wanted to hear it—but instead he was flippant.

And I had to appease both sides. I couldn't tell John off *or* dismiss Carolyn's complaints. Instead, I acted as a mediator, which was instinctual, having spent most of my childhood trying to assuage my mom. That early training made me an expert at finding a rationale for someone else's less-than-perfect behavior. I could always see the other side.

To John, I would say, "Give her a break"; to Carolyn, "He doesn't get it." Seventy percent of the time I was successful in resolving the situation, which is what happened with *George*'s anniversary party at Asia de Cuba. Carolyn actually didn't want to go because she was mad at John for not calling her from the retreat all weekend. I smoothed things over between them, but it left me completely and utterly depleted, as mediating always did.

Once I sorted out the drama and returned from the retreat, I barely had time to shower and change before going to the party. I raced around my apartment, quickly throwing on a dress I bought a week before, and dashed out to hail a cab.

As I sat in the back of the taxi, it dawned on me that I didn't have anyone to ask me how *I* felt. My job didn't leave much room for a life outside *George,* John, and Carolyn. By becoming a protective vault 24/7, I sacrificed my own needs. I couldn't give attention to a relationship of my own, yet I was stuck in the middle of theirs. But as soon as I walked through the doors of the party, I hid behind a big smile. It was all part of the gig.

I hadn't seen Frank in weeks, family gatherings had taken a backseat (my mother would say, "You mean to tell me you aren't coming home *again* for Sunday dinner?"), and I hadn't been on a real date in months. My most important relationship was with John Kennedy, and he just didn't do it for me. By the time I landed at John's place in Hyannis for my weeklong vacation during the summer of 1998, I was spent and looking forward to turning everything off, including my brain.

At 7:30 a.m. the second morning of my vacation, still groggy from Provi's amazing daiquiris the night before, I heard a knock at my door. "Rose, your sister's on the phone." It was Billy Noonan, John's friend, who was also a guest at the house.

When I opened the bedroom door, he wore an unmistakable look of concern. As I made my way to the phone, I passed Provi in the hallway wringing her hands. Phone calls from family that early in the morning were never a good sign. *My father's dead. I just know it,* I thought.

My sister Amy was crying hysterically when I picked up the phone.

"I'm so sorry, RoseMarie," she sobbed.

"Is it Dad?"

"It's not that."

"Oh my God. It's Mom?"

"No, no."

The guessing game was getting on my nerves. "Please tell me what's going on. You're freaking me out!"

"Frank passed away last night."

"Who's Frank?" I asked, puzzled.

"Frank Giordano," my sister said, crying even harder.

"What are you talking about? Frank's on Fire Island. He's not dead."

"RoseMarie, he had a heart attack."

Frank. My Frank. My best friend—the person I spoke to on the phone four times a day, the person who eased me into my new life, the person I loved more than anyone else—was gone. As the realization hit me, I dropped the phone, doubled over, and screamed in horror.

Frank, at thirty-six years old, had died of a drug overdose. I was stunned. It didn't make sense. And yet, just one month earlier, I had received a disturbing message on my answering machine from a state psychiatrist informing Frank that he had missed his court-appointed rehab date. *What the fuck is she*

181

talking about? I wondered. Frank must have gotten into trouble and left my phone number as a contact. I immediately called him and he fessed up.

"I got arrested," he said.

"For what?"

"For possession of cocaine, and I didn't even have that much on me."

I went ballistic. He got arrested for drugs and didn't call me? I worked for JFK Jr. for Christ's sake. I could have called someone to help him out. Instead, Frank had taken the matter into his own hands, choosing rehab over jail time. But, he told me, he didn't want to go because it was filled with depressing homeless heroin addicts. No shit.

Frank wasn't the only one in denial. Despite his run-in with the law, which had escalated into a full-on crisis, I was still ignoring his enduring problem with drugs. I thought he was on the cusp of getting his shit together. About a month earlier, Matt had given Frank a serious, tough-love pep talk at a nondescript hole-in-the-wall Italian restaurant we went to when we didn't want to run into anyone we knew. "Frank, it's ridiculous. You have to get an apartment and move out of your mom's house," Matt said. "Buy an apartment. We know a million people. You're a great person. We can help you make this happen." Frank listened to him. Matt, a success at twenty-nine, introduced Frank to his broker, who found him a perfect one-bedroom on Spring and Bowery for $100,000. He had enough money saved up from his job with Brad Johns to make a down payment, which he did one week before he died.

Why hadn't I insisted Frank come with me to Hyannis? He said his friend had already paid for the room on Fire Island so that they could go to the White Party—a raucous annual beach party to benefit the Gay Men's Health Crisis Center—and he was reluctant to back out at the last minute.

"I don't want to go, but I have to," he said.

"You've been to that party a million times. Come on."

I should have persisted—I knew his going to Fire Island was a bad idea. For as much as I prided myself on my ability to take care of people, I had let down the most important person in my life, the one to whom I owed everything. If not for Frank, I wouldn't have been working for John or living in Manhattan. Ironically, if not for Frank, I wouldn't have grown up and taken responsibility for myself. Unconditionally my champion, he made me feel like I could do anything. He was my confidant and partner in crime. I could murder someone and come to him with the smoking gun, and he would say, "Okay, here's what we need to do." He wouldn't even ask what happened. It wouldn't have mattered.

At the beginning of the summer, Frank and I dog-sat at John's house on Martha's Vineyard and had an amazing weekend: we went skinny-dipping for the first time at the private beach and cooked delicious meals. One night, while we were making dinner in the kitchen, Frank looked up at me and said, "Rosie, you know, this is what it's like to be married. We are as close as any couple."

And now he was gone. I felt like a widow as I threw my clothes into a suitcase and caught a 9:30 a.m. flight out of Hyannis. As I raced to the plane, my body was numb, but my emotions were on overdrive. Sitting in the first seat of the puddle jumper, I couldn't stop sobbing.

"Are you okay, miss?" the passenger next to me asked.

"No, I'm not," I whispered through my tears.

When I got back to my apartment, Nancy, my best friend from high school, was already there. She didn't want me to be alone when I listened to dozens of answering machine messages from the night before. Carolyn arrived a few hours later and insisted we order a pizza. I hadn't consumed anything other than cigarettes all day.

Less than a week later, after a surreal funeral with Frank's inconsolable mom and everyone treating me like his widow, I dove back into work. It felt like all I had left. Although John, who was traveling in Vietnam, would be away for another week, I cut my own vacation short and returned to the office. I was grateful for the enormous pile of mail I found waiting for me. Opening John's mail was how I started every day. The routine was the only thing that felt good that day.

I hadn't made it through a quarter of the letters when John phoned from Vietnam.

"Rosie, I'm so sorry," he said, his voice crackling and thin as if it had traveled to me from the past.

"Thanks," I choked.

"Do you want me to come home?" he asked.

"It's sweet of you to offer, but that's the last thing I want, because it will be about me for five seconds. And then it will be all about you," I said, sort of joking.

I was wrong—when John returned, it wasn't all about him. Although everyone in the office clamored to get a minute with him as soon as they saw him walking down the hallway ("How was your trip, John?" "Let me know when you have a minute. I need to talk to you about something important"), he put his hand up and said, "Not now. Where's Rosie?"

John came right up to me. "Come here," he said, putting his arms around me. "Are you okay?"

"No," I said, and broke down.

He ushered me into his office and closed the door. I sat down and sobbed almost as hard as I had when I first heard the news of Frank's death.

"You have to grieve and mourn, but Frank lived his life the way he wanted to," John said. "The reason he loved you so much was because you accepted him for that. Very few people allow others to live their lives on their own terms. Now that he's gone, don't glamorize or demonize Frank. Remember him for who he really was. If you don't, you will never get past it."

I held on to each of John's words. He knew what he was talking about.

"Whenever there's a tragedy, a tiny nub of green starts to grow inside you. It's a regrowth," John continued. "You have to hold on to that little nub until it grows into the tree that is the next part of your life."

Christmas of 1998 looked like it was going to be a wash for many reasons. With Frank gone, it was sure to be the worst holiday season ever. And now Negi and I had to throw a holiday party on the measly budget Hachette had provided.

"Two hundred and fifty dollars? We can't do anything with that. We should just forget it and give the money to charity," I said. I didn't feel like celebrating this year anyway.

John walked by and, overhearing my last comment, he said, laughing, "I thought *you* were the charity, Rosie."

I ignored him. But after learning about the tiny party budget, he decided to pitch in some money of his own—ten thousand dollars, to be precise.

John's one stipulation for footing the bill was that no one could wear black to the party—a radical request since we all constantly wore black. But ten thousand dollars was ten thousand dollars, and Negi, Biz, and I set about planning a blowout—a DJ, open bar, the works.

In the weeks leading up to the party, I became more and more excited, because this was going to be just that—a party. No expectations. No press. No pressure. We didn't have to appease advertisers or woo celebrities. It was a rare opportunity to have a good time and toast ourselves. And I really needed to have some fun again.

The night did not disappoint. The city twinkled festively outside the wall of windows in the loft space we had rented through Biz's friend. The Puck Building is an old downtown edifice that once housed the satirical monthly *Spy* magazine, which famously poked fun at everything, including *George*. Without any hidden agendas, the *George* staff was more relaxed that night.

Carolyn gave me an enormous hug as soon as she found me in the big, open room. "You are the best-dressed person here," she said, holding me at arm's length to get a full view.

I didn't have a single nonblack item in my closet, so I went shopping and bought a sheer, light-blue sheath with tiny silver sequins. It was gorgeous.

"I love that, of course, you ignored John's rules completely." She wore a black dress.

"Fuck it. I don't care." She laughed. "I don't work for *George*. I can wear black."

For the first time since starting my job, I brought friends other than Frank to a work function. A family friend, an ex-boyfriend, the guy I was having a fling with, and a few other folks came to the party to see my other life and meet John. The staff party was the perfect opportunity to introduce my friends to him. I didn't need to worry that they would act like freaks, say something inappropriate, or tattle to a paper; we could all let our guard down and just enjoy ourselves. And, of course, my friends were thrilled to be invited. The DJ was awesome, too. I was dancing with a friend when Prince's "It's Gonna Be a Beautiful Night" came on and I felt a tug on my elbow. It was John.

"Would you like to dance?" he asked.

"Sure, I'd love to."

He looked amazing in a green velvet Gucci suit that only he could pull off. He grabbed both my hands, which made us laugh. Even in the dim light, I could see his face brighten as we grooved to Prince's soulful singing.

As we danced together, I felt every eye in the room trained on us. Forming a circle, people craned their necks to get a glimpse. It was just John, whom I goofed on every day. And I had spent countless hours making fun of the way other people got swept up by his charm. But in that moment I felt like a princess. It was intentional on John's part. He wanted everyone in that room to know I was special. He was giving me permission to show off by showing me off. And yet it felt as if we were the only two people on the dance floor.

He stopped in the middle of the floor and kissed my hand. "Thank you," he said. "I appreciate everything you do for me. You're my best friend."

The past year had been rough. John and I had each been through a lot, personally and professionally. The stresses of not knowing whether *George* would be in business by next Christmas or what story about him, Carolyn, or the magazine would pop in the press next had left our nerves frayed and exposed. But despite the consuming nature of my work, the ups and downs of the past, and those surely to come, I knew, dancing with John, that I was exactly where I was supposed to be. He wasn't just a boss but someone I truly cared about, and he felt the same way about me. No matter how difficult the subject matter, we were always up-front and honest with each other. Our relationship had started out sincerely, and it never changed. With Frank gone, I had no one else like that in my life.

"John, I just want you to know I really love my job," I said. "Whatever you decide to do, I'm coming with you."

I gave John a hug and a kiss, secure and happy in the knowledge that with him I would always have a job and a life. A great life full of drama, glamour, inside stories, and laughter. I didn't care if we were working at a magazine or selling ties on the street, I wasn't leaving his side.

The day before the Christmas break, I found the usual mountain of lavish gifts on my desk in what had become quite an expensive holiday ritual for Carolyn. She'd bought me scarves and shoes and a purse she had seen me coveting in the window of the Prada store almost a month before. I would have to talk to her about next year—she couldn't keep shopping like this. Especially if *George* went under. But for now I decided to just enjoy it and be grateful.

On top of the pile sat a note from John. While everyone else drank leftover alcohol from the Christmas party in the conference room, I took a moment to myself and opened the card.

Dear Rosey,

I couldn't find any paste so this will have to do. I want to thank you for all your

The Season's Greetings

and best wishes for the New Year

help over the past year but particularly for your toughness, savvy and loyalty to me, Carolyn and George. Though you wouldn't know it, you have grown <u>tremendously</u> in the past year into a remarkable and formidable woman. You should be very proud of you. I am (You're not a bad marriage counselor either) Enjoy! With affection, admiration and gratitude.

JOHN

CHAPTER
10

—

"What's wrong?" I asked John, who I could tell was upset.

"Carolyn has decided she's not coming to Rory's wedding," he said, standing at the round table in his office where I piled the mail, looking through his papers without reading them.

John's cousin Rory, the youngest of Robert Kennedy's children, was getting married at her mother's home in Hyannis that Saturday. The entire Kennedy family was gathering; if Carolyn didn't show, it would raise eyebrows. Not to mention the endless speculation that would occur when the press got wind of it.

"You know how she is. She'll put up a stink and say she's not going, but she's going to go," I assured him.

"No, she's not. She's determined to stay home this weekend, and I'm not going to fight with her about it."

Okay. Here we go. I would have to step in and make sure

191

the disagreement didn't get overblown. "You're not going to the wedding alone."

I was annoyed that nowadays I always seemed to be playing referee. The constant scrutiny of their marriage had taken a toll. Where they once laughed off problems or misunderstandings, they now blew them out of proportion and were both too stubborn to work things out on their own. When they were acting like twelve-year-olds who needed an adult to take charge, it was easier for me just to try to make peace than to deal with the fallout. This was a couple that wasn't allowed to just have a normal fight and move on.

As much as I wanted to solve another problem for John, I felt for Carolyn. While the press was interested in them as a couple, they were relentless with her. No matter how private she and John were in their personal lives, the media wouldn't stop hounding her. The stories, the speculation, and the meanness toward her never wavered.

In the past three years, the press had Carolyn getting divorced, becoming anorexic, being cheated on, cheating. Sometimes she was pregnant and sometimes she couldn't get pregnant. Photographers followed her everywhere, including to the gynecologist's office. In fact, when the paparazzo tailing her one afternoon realized she had entered the office of an ob-gyn, he knew he hit pay dirt. He took a picture of the plaque outside the office with all the doctors' names. Because the practice had a fertility specialist, the newspaper, which ran a picture of the plaque, concocted a story that Carolyn was having trouble conceiving.

That was familiar territory for the tabloids, but even respected journalists went after Carolyn. Somehow, it was perfectly acceptable for publications such as the *New York Times,* *New York* magazine, and *Newsweek* to make disparaging remarks about her personality based on nothing more than how she looked in photos. *Newsweek* printed that "Carolyn . . . has the public persona of a vaguely soulless mannequin." Maureen Dowd wrote an insulting article in the *New York Times* painting Carolyn as a "cunning" woman who shared the blame for turning the serious Kennedys superficial. She quoted Edward Klein, the author of a number of books on the Kennedys—or, as John called him, "a guy who had lunch with my mother twenty years ago and has been dining out on it ever since"—who described Carolyn and John as "a 90's couple, all image and no substance. The content is gone." Over and over, people said the same thing: Carolyn wasn't good enough for John.

Besides having to deal with the public criticism, she also felt the pressure of being the caretaker in John's big life. Something grave was always happening—such as the battle with cancer that John's cousin and best friend Anthony Radziwill seemed to be on the verge of losing. Anthony was like the brother John never had. Each the best man at the other's wedding, Anthony and John spent almost every summer weekend together on Martha's Vineyard. It went past family; they enjoyed each other's company despite their mutual merciless teasing (one of Anthony's favorite jokes was to call the office and offer me a job at HBO, where he worked).

No matter the problem, Carolyn played the cheerleader, propping John up. She was the one at the hospital with Anthony while John worked late into the night at the magazine, and she would have to pick up the pieces if Anthony died. "John, we're going to get through this," I heard her say many times. "It's going to be okay."

And now the newest crisis: *George* had lost its publisher. Hachette began severing ties when David Pecker jumped ship to take a job running American Media—the *National Enquirer* publisher. (It was ironic that Pecker now put out a magazine that hounded John and Carolyn relentlessly, which I didn't find very funny, although John did.) While Pecker had long put pressure on John to bring up *George*'s numbers, he'd also been the one to decide to publish it in the first place, so he'd had a vested interest in its success. After his surprising departure, *George*'s future with Hachette became even more tenuous.

Then in June 1999, John returned to the office after a meeting with Hachette's new CEO, Jack Kliger. He had a smirk on his face when he motioned for me to come into his office.

"So Jack told me they're not going forward with *George*," he said, still grinning.

Had John finally lost it? Why the hell was he smiling after getting such bad news?

"We'll be all right," I said reassuringly. I could never act upset, because my role was to make him feel okay about everything at work, just as Carolyn did for him at home.

"Kliger didn't even have to say it," John said, starting to laugh. "You know how I knew? When I went into his office, I put my water bottle on his desk. And he was so nervous, he picked up *my* water bottle and started drinking from it."

While the verdict wasn't a surprise, it was a setback for John, who refused to accept failure for the magazine. *Vanity Fair* had taken six years to become profitable, but because John was behind *George,* people expected miracles. John felt the solution was to find another partner. Determined to keep *George* going in some shape or form, John had already begun to raise money and had sunk some of his own capital into its next incarnation. "This magazine has to be a success; otherwise I can't move on to the next venture, whatever that may be," he said. He was in "let's roll up our sleeves and figure it out" mode. The hunt for new investors took its toll on John, but he remained upbeat, declaring to the staff, "We *will* find a new home."

Carolyn knew it was up to her to feed his optimism.

But what about her? When would life calm down and give them a little breathing room to focus on their marriage and enjoy each other? Never, it seemed. Now that John had to find new investors for *George* and build his business anew, there was no end in sight.

At her wit's end, Carolyn began to act out—not showing up to a lunch date with John or going out for cocktails without letting him know where she was. Worried sick, John would call me to see if I knew her whereabouts. "Oh, she's probably just blowing you off like you've done to her a million times," I would say, trying to make light of the situation.

But there was nothing funny about backing out of a Kennedy wedding at the last minute. Magazine editors, perusing the paparazzi offerings, would mark her absence. The follow-up coverage would be never-ending and nasty—and once again my job to manage.

Time for an intervention.

"John, I need to have a little chat with your wife in private." I stood up, indicating my intention to take his seat and call her from his office.

He walked out, not looking in my direction.

I sat in his chair, gazing out over the buildings baking in the July heat, and picked up the receiver. I wasn't nervous about confronting Carolyn. I loved Carolyn like a sister, and sometimes sisters argue. It wouldn't be the first time we fought.

Carolyn had started acting weird after I hired an assistant in May. My having some permanent help had been a long time coming. In the past year, I had taken on a bigger role at the magazine, as well as overseeing the marketing and PR departments at *George*—not to mention John's personal media requests. My obligations had grown so much that I could no longer manage smaller tasks, such as ordering lunch or arranging car service pickups.

I had Matt Cowen, the most loyal and competent intern ever, but when he was hired as an associate editor, I had to find someone. After an arduous hiring process (it was difficult to find someone who wouldn't walk in and throw up on themselves because they were in the presence of John Kennedy), I finally found Debbie, a sweet, down-to-earth woman in her late twenties with a great work ethic who was excited to be a second assistant.

Unfortunately, many of those smaller tasks were for Carolyn. "Let Debbie do that," John would say. As my time to talk on the phone or hang out with her shrank, Carolyn was feeling increasingly isolated: her life wasn't her own. She didn't have a job to distract her, and Carolyn was a woman who was used to working. She still hoped to return to a career. But what? There were a lot of stipulations. She couldn't go near fashion because of John's magazine, and she also had to be available to him and his unpredictable life. Not to mention that Carolyn's high-profile presence would have disrupted most offices.

Shortly after Debbie started handling things for her, I could feel Carolyn pulling away when I did reach out. She didn't pick up, like she usually did, when I called and started speaking into the answering machine.

Then one day, John came in and said, "Carolyn asked if you could call the house only when you have to and not randomly."

"Really?" I snapped. "Then, John, don't call *my* house unless it's about work and tell Carolyn the same."

I couldn't believe he was saying that to me after I had worked so hard for so long, devoting every ounce of my energy to *George,* John, and Carolyn. My response was insubordinate (after all, John was my boss), but it was exactly the rise John had hoped for.

"I'm glad you're pissed off at her. You should tell her exactly how you feel," he said, leaving me to stop the bullshit with Carolyn, which I did.

John and Carolyn were unfair to make me responsible for a dynamic I didn't create. Now, with the situation brewing over Rory's wedding, I had more crap to deal with. But so went the life of RoseMarie Terenzio from John Kennedy's office. I picked up the phone to call Carolyn and got right to the heart of the matter.

"Carolyn, are you fucking kidding me?" I said. "What are you doing? You're smarter than this."

"I'm not a priority," she said. "It's always something else. *George.* Somebody getting fired. An event. A trip to Italy to meet advertisers."

"I know. But now's not the time to take a stand. His whole

family's going to be at this wedding, and you need to go with him."

I had readied myself for an argument, but Carolyn didn't offer one. Instead of getting angry, she softened. My chewing her out meant someone realized that she needed some propping up, too—even if it came with a dose of tough love.

"I just want some normal married time," she said. "I'm exhausted."

I thought back on all the times my mom had told me and my sisters, "In my next life, I'm going to raise poodles instead of kids." Hearing Carolyn pine for normalcy reminded me that although they were the most famous people on the planet, Carolyn and John were going through the same problems as anyone else, the normal trials of marriage and family. They could work it out. But first I had to get her to attend this wedding.

"Listen, Carolyn. You don't want to put John in a position where he has to explain where you are, and you don't want to put yourself in a position of being judged," I said. "You get enough of that."

"I don't have anything to wear."

"Go get a dress, and I'll get you a car to the airport."

I was relieved when Carolyn agreed to go. It was one less thing to worry about.

I pulled an open bottle of white wine from John and Carolyn's refrigerator and poured myself a huge glass. It was nearly midnight on the Friday of the longest week ever. Although John and Carolyn had left together for Rory's wedding, I still wasn't done working. While sipping my wine, I was on the phone with Matt Berman, giving him an idea from John for the Rob Lowe cover shoot happening in L.A. the next day. John had a very specific image in mind: he wanted the actor—who was caught on videotape having sex with two women (one of whom was underage) before the Democratic National Convention in 1998, where he was campaigning for Michael Dukakis—to be in a repentant pose, holding rosary beads. The peg for the story was Rob Lowe's new TV show *The West Wing,* which revolved around the White House. As I gave John's notes to Matt, I sipped my wine in the silence of the loft's large interior and began to wind down from a particularly stressful day.

Despite having spent countless hours hanging out in John and Carolyn's apartment, I'd never stayed there overnight or alone. But John had offered me their place because my air conditioner was broken. Earlier that afternoon, after overhearing me in the office calling around for a repairman, he leaned on the doorframe, crossing his arms, his shirtsleeves rolled up, looking at me like *Are you kidding me?*

"Rosie, no one in Manhattan is going to fix your air conditioner on a Friday afternoon when it's nine thousand degrees outside."

Even John, who could get anything he wanted with a snap of his fingers, knew when to accept the impossible.

"Stay at our place," he said. "There's food and wine in the fridge. Besides, Carolyn would kill me if she knew I let you suffocate in your apartment all weekend."

And just like that, my problem disappeared. That was John. He fixed everything, or at least gave me some peace of mind. But he quickly followed his magnanimous gesture with a wisecrack:

"Just don't sit around sniffing my clothes," he said. "I know you want to, because you're so in love with me."

Soon after, John popped his head in again to tell me he was going to work out and then head off for the weekend.

"You have to meet Lauren in the lobby at six-thirty," I said.

John was flying his plane to Massachusetts and dropping Carolyn's sister off for a weekend on Martha's Vineyard before continuing on with Carolyn to Hyannis.

After reminding John to pick up Lauren, I said, "Do you mind if I leave at five-thirty today?"

"Sure, Rosie, no problem. I'll call you later."

As he walked out the door, he turned to me once more and said, "Rosie, you're the best. Thanks for smoothing things over."

Before I left for the day, I put a pink sticky note on the table in his office: "Meet Lauren in the lobby at 6:30." It never hurt to remind John twice.

A little after midnight—while I was tying up the main line talking to Matt—the fax line started ringing. The loft didn't have call waiting, because Carolyn hated it—she thought it was rude to put someone on hold to find out who else was calling. (Whenever people, frustrated by a very persistent busy signal, asked why they didn't have call waiting, I would say, "They can't afford it.")

Probably only five people in the world had the fax number, so when I heard it ring that late, I figured it was John or Carolyn calling to check in. I told Matt I'd call him back and picked up the fax line.

"Hello," I said.

"Oh, Carolyn, thank God you're home."

It was Carole Radziwill, Anthony's wife.

"Carole, it's Rose. What's going on?"

"Where are they?" Carole asked.

"What do you mean, where are they?"

The friend who was supposed to pick John and Carolyn up in Hyannis had called the house on the Vineyard—they didn't arrive at the airport. Carole, who was spending the summer with Anthony at John's house, had been frantically trying Carolyn's cell phone, all the while hoping the busy signal at the loft meant they had never left the city. Realizing they weren't at home, she released a small "Oh God."

No way. No fucking way. I hadn't understood the direness of the situation until Carole uttered those words, but I refused to let my mind wander anywhere near the vicinity of their meaning. *No way.* Working for John came with a host of expectations and responsibilities: dealing with the media, maintaining his privacy, and making his life run as smoothly as possible. Being prepared for the unexpected had been part of the job, and I had always risen to the occasion. I could deal with anything. But not this.

There has got to be an explanation other than the obvious one. There's no way that John would let something like this happen. They're fine. They just decided not to go. They went someplace else, that's all. I will find them.

I had to get off the phone and find out what happened. I had to fix this. Carole had already called the airports in Hyannis and on the Vineyard, so I called his flight instructor, Jay Biederman. I woke up his roommate, who told me Jay was on vacation with his family in Switzerland. I didn't care where the fuck he was; I needed to find him. He'd know what was going on. I terrified the roommate, who dug up a number. It didn't matter that he was overseas or that it was so early in the morning there; when I reached Jay, he heard the panic in my voice and reassured me: "He's done it so many times by himself, and it's such a short flight. He hugs the coastline the whole way." We were in agreement: no way had the plane gone down. Things like that just did not happen.

I thought about my last conversation with Carolyn and how I'd told her to get on the plane. *Oh God.* Standing alone in the middle of that big, empty space, I made phone call after phone call. Smoking a thousand cigarettes, I called the airports—Caldwell, Hyannis, Martha's Vineyard. I called Ted Kennedy's house in Hyannis and his assistant at home. I called the friends who were supposed to pick them up, and I called Matt.

I needed to stop Matt from going to L.A. for the Rob Lowe shoot. He had to be here. But I kept getting his answering machine. He had probably turned the ringer off because of his early flight.

I needed to keep it together. When everything sorted itself out in the morning, I didn't want John lighting into me for losing my head and calling the whole world to say his plane was missing. I never wavered from protecting his privacy.

But around 2:00 a.m., Carole called back: she had alerted the Coast Guard.

Oh my God, what is she doing? He is going to kill me. If this becomes a thing, he will be furious with me.

I managed crises and kept things quiet: that was my job. My job *was* John, and I refused to let go.

Just as a sleepless night ended, I finally got Matt on the phone. "Don't go to the airport," I said. "John's plane is missing."

Matt was silent for a long time; then he said only "This is going to be terrible."

My stomach dropped at his verdict. *You don't know that,* I thought.

Having exhausted all my options, I finally turned on the television to see what the news was reporting. CNN showed footage of military helicopters scanning the dark waters around Martha's Vineyard. The monstrous picture on the screen conflicted with an image that continued to run through my mind, consoling me like an old family photo, of John landing in a field and exiting the plane, a dirt-streaked Carolyn, angry but unhurt, not far behind.

The phone wouldn't stop ringing, with every friend, family member, and colleague who had the number calling the apartment. I engaged in that irrational communication, answering the phone each time as if I were simply taking down a message while John and Carolyn were out of town, like any good houseguest. But people wanted answers, and I didn't have them.

I tried to ground myself by checking my home machine—remembering there was another place I belonged—and discovered I had dozens of messages.

"Rose, I am so sorry," each message began.

Fuck that. They hadn't even found the plane yet and people were ready to give up on him. Well, I wasn't. I hung up the phone. But as soon as I did, it rang again. I picked up. I had to: it could be John needing help. Of course, it wasn't.

At seven o'clock in the morning, one call came in that I was glad to get. It was Carolyn's best friend, Jessica, who had become a judgment-free, safe harbor for anything to do with Carolyn.

"Jessica," I said. "You need to come down here right away."

She hung up before I had finished my sentence and was at the door so fast I swear she must have flown.

"Where is she?" Jessica, still wearing her pajamas, asked when I opened the door.

"What do you mean, where is she?" I asked.

Jessica had lent a sympathetic ear to Carolyn the day she refused to go to Rory's wedding and hadn't spoken to her since my intervention. She assumed I was keeping Carolyn company as she hid at home freaking out about John.

"She went with him, Jessica," I said.

Jessica lost it. She cried. I cried. We reminisced, and then scolded ourselves for it. We schemed, and then were embarrassed. We were all over the place. How else could we be? No blueprint existed for behavior in such a situation. Having Jessica as company was a relief, but eventually she had to go back home. She had a life. *Unlike me,* I thought, and then pushed it out of my mind. *This is just a big mistake.*

After she left, I was alone again, inundated with phone calls and overwhelmed by the solemn droning of the TV. I wanted to rip the phone out of the wall and throw the television out the window. An hour later, the intercom rang. It was Tony, a friend of John's whom I had called at 6:00 a.m. because he owned the gym where John worked out—one of the last places he went before getting on the plane. I thought he might be able to provide me with a clue to help me find John. After I tracked him down in the Hamptons, Tony told me he was coming back to the city right away.

As soon as he walked through the front door, I fell into his arms and sobbed uncontrollably. A deep well of abandonment poured out—John and Carolyn disappeared, and nobody believed they were coming back. A strong, macho Italian guy, Tony immediately stepped into the role of my protector, which I so desperately wanted and needed in that moment.

His visit was also a reality check, as I listened to his description of the media and mourners gathered outside the building; I shivered as I realized I had no idea what was going on in the outside world, even nine floors down. Apparently, hundreds of people had appeared to leave flowers and candles and to pay their respects. So many had assembled that the police put up barriers to make an organized line for those wishing to visit the makeshift memorial. That was in addition to the hundreds of media outlets stationed on the block.

After the news programs began listing the date of John and Carolyn's deaths—July 16, 1999—before the Coast Guard had even made the announcement, I turned off the television and went into a media blackout. It was death porn and I couldn't look at it. I popped in a videotape, Chris Rock's comedy special *Bring the Pain,* and played it on a loop. It was my salvation.

Day turned into night without notice. The calls that never stopped coming allowed me to ignore the passage of time, Saturday becoming Saturday night, hope becoming hopelessness. Tony kept urging me to take a break, put the phone down, but I wouldn't hear of it. He said I needed to eat—a typical Italian response to tragedy. Nicotine was all the fuel I needed. And rage.

One phone call in particular got me so angry I could feel my mother's influence (the part of me that could tell off a bishop in church) asserting itself.

"RoseMarie, it's Barbara Walters. Can you ever forgive me for calling you at a time like this?"

How the hell did she get that number, and how did she know I was at John and Carolyn's? I wanted to kill the person who gave her the information.

"Probably not," I answered.

"I'm going on the air tonight with *20/20*. I already have people who are going to talk to me. Is there any way you can say something, on or off the record?"

"Anyone who is going to come on the air tonight doesn't know anything and is not a close friend of John's. Trust me," I said before hanging up.

I could deal with scandal, problems at *George*, or Carolyn being stalked, but not this. I didn't know how to do this.

Around dinnertime, the intercom rang again. Downstairs, Richie Notar, one of the owners of Nobu, had beat his way through the sobbing mourners, bushels of flowers, a cathedral's worth of candles, and pushy paparazzi to deliver bags and bags filled with food. Nobody told him to come, he just came, figuring someone would be here, trapped and in need of nourishment. He didn't start eulogizing John, a regular at his restaurant, which was around the corner from the loft, and someone he worked out with at the gym; he just dropped off the bags of food. I practically choked on his kindness before giving him a huge hug. Delivering a five-star meal to a woman holding a vigil was the kind of thing John would do.

After Richie left, Tony set the table and started to lay out all the gorgeous food.

"RoseMarie, come sit," he said softly.

I looked at the food covering the table and it turned my

stomach. The phone rang again and I lunged for it. "Hello?" I said desperately.

Tony wrenched the phone from my hand and hung it up.

"You don't need to talk to whoever that is," he said. "Now sit. And eat."

He took me by the shoulders and guided me to the table as if I were a child. We sat in silence, me picking at my food, and him devouring the meal as if he had just completed a marathon workout.

The phone continued to ring throughout dinner and as we cleared the dishes. It rang while we sat on the couch through another round of *Bring the Pain*. And it rang through the night. But somehow, having Tony there—someone just there for me—I was able to let go and sleep for a few hours.

In the wee hours of Sunday morning, when the phone rang again, I picked it up by force of habit. *John, call, you asshole.*

It was Senator Kennedy's office. In a tight, quiet voice, his aide relayed the message that the Coast Guard had changed the status of its mission from search and rescue to search and recovery.

"What does that mean?" I asked.

"They don't expect to find them alive," she said.

As the predawn light began to etch out the details of their belongings—hats, a chair, framed photographs, books, a pair of shoes, all so ordinary and unfeeling—I knew with certainty. John and Carolyn were gone.

A week after a single phone call sent my life crashing to pieces, I couldn't face John and Carolyn's funeral alone. The day was cruelly hot. *Thank God for air-conditioning.* I thought as Negi and I rode uptown together for support. I put my head against the black leather of the car's headrest, but I couldn't relax. Details ran through my head: faxes of reading assignments for the funeral, messages from out-of-town guests, addresses for invitations to the service. Although John and Carolyn were gone, my work for them was ongoing. Just as I had dealt with the logistics of their lives, so did I continue to after their deaths. At the request of the families, I had spent the past week in the apartment, amid their belongings and their memories, which I wrapped around myself like a security blanket. Tony stayed by my side, making me coffee in the morning, going off to work, and returning in the evening with takeout or groceries. I didn't say it out loud, but I secretly hoped our friendship would lead to something more. During that crazy time, he made sense: a tough Italian business owner and a friend of John's. How perfect.

I helped Caroline plan the funeral at St. Thomas More, the church she and John had attended as kids. Up until that point, my relationship with John's sister had consisted of niceties on the phone and at a few dinner parties. In the past week, however, I had gone through Rolodexes, helped her compile a list of attendees, and then dealt with the RSVPs. We bonded over the absurdity of John being gone and how much he would have hated the hoopla over his death.

"Don't you feel like he's going to get angry at us for letting this whole thing get so out of control?" Caroline said in a sentiment shockingly close to my own.

"Yes!" I said. "I think he's going to come back and yell at me for giving away his Bruce Springsteen tickets."

Like John's life, his funeral was a complicated affair. The small church on 89th Street and Madison Avenue couldn't accommodate all those who wanted to say good-bye, and I knew many who weren't invited would be offended beyond repair. For the most part, I kept my mouth shut as Caroline removed people from the list, but I protested when she told me I could pick only five people from *George* to attend the funeral.

"Caroline, I can't do that," I said. "There will be people sitting in that church who didn't give your brother credit for running a magazine—and I think it's time they did. The staff needs to be there."

I'm sure she was taken aback by my bold stance, but what did I have left to lose?

"I think we have to invite everybody from the magazine, or no one," I said. "And that includes me."

Caroline said she had to think about it. But she called me later to let me know I could invite everyone from *George*.

While the car zipped up Madison Avenue, I looked out at all the shops that at one point in my life I wouldn't have dared to go into without Carolyn. The clothes in the windows sparkled in a bright blur of wasted color. Then, all of a sudden, we hit an ugly snarl of traffic at 72nd Street. Cabbies, wedged in between public buses and bewildered out-of-town drivers, leaned on their horns. Traffic this far uptown, especially at this time of day, was unusual.

"I've got to get to a funeral," I pleaded with the driver.

He made a quick turn and raced down the block toward Park Avenue, but at the end of the street were police barricades blocking the avenue. *Today of all days, they had to close down Park Avenue? Just what I need right now.* As we approached, a lump began to form in my throat as the officers shook their heads and waved at us to back up.

Negi ran out of the car and up to the cops, waving the invitation to John's funeral as if it were a badge.

"Can you let us through?" she pleaded. "This is John Kennedy's assistant. We're going to the funeral and can't be late. She's got to read something."

"I can't let you through," the cop said. "But get in and we'll take you."

Negi and I hopped into the back of a cop car as if it were something we did every day and zipped uptown on the empty avenue.

"What's going on, anyway? Why's Park Avenue closed?" I asked, calming down now that we were getting a police escort. The officer looked at me like I was crazy.

"It's for John's funeral."

Of course. John was someone whose life—and now death—was shared by the world.

"I feel like a perp sitting back here," I said, trying to change the subject.

"What do you know about perps?" the cop in the passenger seat said.

"From John's days at the DA's office, he used to say, 'Perps don't die. You can shoot a cop once and he'll be dead on the spot. You shoot a perp twenty times and he'll live.'"

The cop laughed. "That's true!" Then he turned around to look at me. "I'm really sorry," he said. "The whole city is in mourning today."

It took everything inside me to keep from breaking down. John was a New York City fixture. When I realized how much John meant to all kinds of people, just like the cop, the loss grew even larger.

The police dropped us off outside St. Thomas More, where a media circus had assembled, every outlet in the world vying for the best position to film the somber dignitaries as they entered the church. Inside, people came up to me asking me where they should sit. *Where should you sit?* I wanted to say. *Don't worry about where you're sitting. It's a funeral, not a cocktail party.*

The endless jockeying around John, even in a moment like that, made me sick. It was as if the church pews had become social strata. I could tend to the mourners, tell them what to do and where to go, but I didn't want to work right then. I wanted to scream: *I'm not just an assistant. I'm a mourner, too.* Not being a family member, childhood friend, or college buddy, I felt alone in my grief.

The organizers had wanted me to sit up front with the people reading passages, but I stuck close to the members of *George* who had shown up to honor their boss. They anchored me as I watched my life drift away on the backs of eulogies and tears. Tony, who stood in the back of the church as a pallbearer, found me with his eyes.

When I walked to the front of the church to give my reading, past every single Kennedy, past President Clinton, his wife, Hillary, and daughter, Chelsea, my knees were shaking to the point where I didn't think they would hold me. That sense of duty to John, which had defied my skepticism in the beginning and had supported me through the ups and downs of his life, pushed me forward.

*   *   *

Back inside John and Carolyn's apartment a week after the funeral, I couldn't hear if the paparazzi were still waiting for famous faces to appear, or whether mourners continued to leave flowers at the makeshift shrine. None of the street noise that penetrates a typical New York City apartment interrupted my isolation. The silence was different from the first frenetic days after the crash, when the phone and fax lines refused to stop ringing—an endless loop of calls placed, received, returned, and missed. While the Coast Guard searched the unyielding water, I had a purpose—to disseminate information. But now I faced only silence. More than anything, the silence forced me to come to terms with the reality that John and Carolyn were gone. Their day planners had always been crammed with friends and obligations. Now there were only empty pages.

I don't remember who asked me to pack up their things, probably Caroline, but it made sense. I had run John's life for the past five years. Nobody was close to him in quite the same way I was. Of course, he had countless friends and relatives, but they all had lives of their own. I, on the other hand, was with him every day, all day. So why wouldn't I be here now?

Still, I didn't feel right dismantling their lives. But I did it because I was the only person who could. I tended to the practical stuff first, such as cleaning out their fridge: emptying the fruit, tossing the Gatorade and white wine. I pulled the vodka and ice cream out of the freezer and threw it in the trash. I moved on to the bedroom—which was furnished with a big bed, two nightstands, a television, and a pair of dressers with a few photos of them together—and laid items from the closet and drawers on the bed.

The closet was divided into two sides, one for her and the other for him. Carolyn was very organized, and she kept John's side neat, too. She always picked up after him. When he came out of the bathroom after showering, she yelled, "John! Three wet towels on the floor!"

She didn't have an enormous wardrobe, but everything she had was beautiful: sumptuous cashmere sweaters, sleek pencil skirts, formfitting sheath dresses, and incredible shoes. Carolyn shopped in high-end stores, but she wasn't excessive with her purchases, and she didn't go to fashion shows and order trunks filled with clothes. She edited herself mercilessly and wore mostly black, navy, and gray. It was relatively easy to pack up her side of the closet.

Cleaning out John's side was much more arduous. I pulled out his shoes, then his T-shirts. Going through his hats was the worst part of the process. He had so many beloved, goofy hats— wool hats, caps, berets, the pom-pom hat he wore the first time I met him at PR/NY. They say the shoes define the man, but in John's case, it was his hats. Not surprisingly, his sister, Caroline, gave them to the women John had been close with.

He also had many beautiful ties. Those Caroline parceled out to the men in John's life.

I tried not to think about John as I pored through his clothes; otherwise, I would never be able to get through it. I contained my grief then the same way I had while helping Caroline plan the funeral. But memories, of course, flooded my mind as I touched his things: My favorite tie, navy blue with a wonderful, bright green pattern. And one of his suits, a navy Zegna with chalky blue pinstripes. I remembered when he first wore it, for a meeting.

"You look gorgeous in that suit," I'd said. It was one of only a handful of times I told him he looked handsome.

"Whoa," he said. "What did you say?"

"If you wore a red tie, it would be very 'John F. Kennedy Jr.,'" I sassed, bringing us back to our usual selves—the Bronx Upstart messing with the Most Famous Man in the World.

With every happy memory, a dark shadow followed close behind. A lurking fear. *John, how dare you leave me here.* I didn't know what would happen to me or where I would go now that he had disappeared. Once his things were packed, I didn't have a job. I didn't have anything. I would be starting all over again and I was terrified. I felt silly and selfish for thinking such things, but I had devoted myself to buoying his successes, holding his secrets, and cleaning up his messes. In return, he looked out for me and brought me into a world that few would ever experience. Now I didn't know whom to turn to. Frank being gone made it even worse. He was the first person I would have turned to in this situation. I could picture him standing in the kitchen while I packed, mixing drinks and telling me things would be okay. Instead, I moved around the apartment completely alone.

CHAPTER
11

A padlock on John's office greeted me when I returned the Monday after he passed away. Death had quickly and easily shut out everything I'd worked for over the past five years.

I had ordered the lock put on because John's office contained priceless objects: a framed flag that Neil Armstrong had taken along on his historic mission to the moon; a document with the original signatures of every president up to his dad; a note from Andrew Jackson; and a paper signed by Abraham Lincoln. Also, I quickly realized, anything belonging to John could become an auction item.

Mike Showalter, the head of facilities for Hachette and a saint, had left a message on my work phone over the weekend saying he and his people were available for "whatever you need." They were devastated; John had always been nice to them. "We'll sit outside your office all day if you need us to," he said.

Instead, I had him put on the padlock, which I now faced as if it were the grim marker of a crime scene.

By contrast, around my desk only a few steps away, flowers spilled from every surface and halfway down the hallway. I couldn't believe how many floral arrangements were there. They covered my desk, chair, floor, and windowsill in a bright, lively display that, like the padlock, only reminded me of John's absence.

I could hardly move because of all the flowers, but I pushed them aside, determined to sit at my desk and open the notes. *That's my job. Open the mail.* The first rule of working for John was not to let his mail pile up or I would never get through it. I had opened his correspondence every morning without fail for the past five years. Today would be no different.

Except today, the notes were addressed to me. I was shocked. I was so used to John being the recipient of the messages that I didn't realize so many people understood what I did and how close I was to him.

Liz Rosenberg
Senior Vice President
Publicity

July 21, 1999

Dear Rose Marie:

I'm so sorry about the loss of your guy. I wanted to just send you my deepest
sympathy and prayers at this terribly sad time for you. I hope it's some
comfort to you knowing that he had someone as wonderful as you taking care
of him while he was here on earth. If I could express this better I would. I
guess I just want you to know I'm thinking about you and I hope you'll try to
be strong.

Love,

Liz R.

Liz Rosenberg, Madonna's publicist.

BRUCE TRACY

7/19

Dear RoseMarie —
You've been on my mind
all weekend. I know there's nothing
one can say at a horrible time like
this. That John valued, admired,
and cared about you has always
been abundantly clear.
Call us if you need us —
Sincerely, Bruce

Bruce Tracy, editor of two books published by *George* magazine: *The Book of Political Lists* and *250 Ways to Make America Better*.

TO: ROSEMARIE TERENZIO
FROM: TERRY and BOB DOLAN SMITH

We haven't had the TV on since Saturday afternoon when there was still that faintest hope.

Terry and I know you are grieving but we hope you are taking immense solace in the quiet knowledge that you WERE John Kennedy Jr. in so many ways. It was your subtle guidance, your consul, and, in the very best sense of the word, your "mothering" which helped the world see the very best John Kennedy. We know how much he relied on you and as scores of lesser others scramble to the heat of the camera to pontificate on every aspect of a John Kennedy they barely knew, WE, and I am sure many others, know who was really there for John.

All the very best.

Bob Dolan Smith

Bob Dolan Smith, a writer for Johnny Carson for twenty years, then for Jay Leno.

I didn't think anyone knew who I was, yet all those people, whom knew John well, took the time to send me their condolences. Some more eloquently than others (Joey sent me a mixed tape with a note on a torn-out piece of notebook paper):

Dear RoseMarie,   8/27/99

I know you are being strong through this hard time. Your strength is in my thoughts and in my heart.

Made this tape for you, hope you dig it.

Much love

Self-pity, which I had yet to let myself feel, expressed itself in silent tears as I continued sorting through the mountain of cards. When the phone rang, any normal person would have let it go to voice mail, but, accustomed to answering, I instinctively picked it up.

"Random Ventures," I said, even as I thought: *There is no more Random Ventures.*

"Is this RoseMarie?" a familiar voice said.

"Yes."

"Do you know who this is?" he asked.

I wasn't in the mood for games. "No," I replied.

"You hear my voice every day on the radio and you don't know who I am?"

I almost died. It was Howard Stern.

Even after we moved to the Hachette building, I kept Howard's show on at the office. At first John made fun of me, but soon enough he was hanging around my desk to listen for a few minutes, or if I was laughing at a joke he'd missed, he asked, "What's Howard talking about today?"

When I first suggested that John put Howard on the cover of *George,* he was skeptical. But I convinced him that Howard had the same mission as the magazine: to bring up important issues by way of entertainment.

Going to the cover shoot was a major perk for me, and John came along—which wasn't his usual MO—because he knew what an important event it was for me. I was extremely nervous, worse than anything I had ever experienced, even on my first day of work. That was the biggest celebrity moment in my life.

When Howard arrived on set, tall and perfect, Matt Berman brought him directly over to the couch where I was sitting.

"This is John's assistant," Matt said. "She's the reason you're on the cover."

I wanted to die right there.

"So I hear you have a crush on me," Howard said. "You work for JFK Jr. and you have a crush on *me*? What's wrong with you?"

I didn't speak or even look at him. I was too scared.

"That's because Rosie's a loser," John said.

"Well, I don't know about that," Howard said.

I was so tongue-tied that I couldn't even tell him about how I excoriated John when I first met him because he had ripped my head shot of Howard. It was all I could do to stand up when he put out his arms for a hug. Then he said, "Will you go on a date with me?"

"Yes, of course I will," I said in a tiny voice.

When the issue was set to hit newsstands, John decided to go on Howard's show to promote the cover, because the King of All Media had been the only on-air celebrity who didn't make his cover participation contingent on John appearing on his radio program. "I feel like I owe it to him," John said. "He was such a gentleman." Hachette's PR people and Nancy Haberman were very distressed, but John told them he could handle it. I was elated.

The morning of the show, Carolyn called me at six, when the program began, and we sat together on the phone listening to the radio.

"I'm so nervous," Carolyn said.

"So am I."

"*What?* Don't say that! I thought you said you weren't nervous about him going on the show."

"No, no. He'll be fine," I said. I was *really* nervous. Howard had an unmatched ability to make people look stupid.

Howard, a total genius, questioned John about all the taboo topics *and* had his famous guest laughing. He even referenced the "Brawl in the Park," a videotaped fight between John and Carolyn when they were still dating that had earned a paparazzo a six-figure paycheck and made my life miserable for the entire week it aired on *Hard Copy*.

"You're dating the hottest chick and you're fighting? Why

are you fighting with her? Over a dog? If she were my girlfriend, I would say, 'You want the dog? Take the dog. Take my hand with the dog.'"

Carolyn laughed into the phone and said, "Oh my God. I love him now."

John was comfortable sitting in Howard's studio because he and Howard weren't that different. Both had outsize personas (albeit dissimilar types) and were fundamentally good guys.

"I'm so sorry. What a tragedy," Howard said to me on the phone the Monday after John died. "If you need anything, you call me."

Although I appreciated Howard's sentiment (Howard Stern wanted to help *me*), I was a bottomless pit of need to the point where no one could help. Without John around to protect me, I felt vulnerable. I wasn't the only one.

That same Monday, Jack Kliger assembled the staff of *George* and addressed John's death with all the sensitivity of a serial killer. I didn't blame him—who was prepared to handle something like this?—but his speech to us was: "We don't know what's going to happen with the magazine. I wish I could tell you, but we just don't know. This is a business, and for now, we have to keep going." We were still trying to process what had happened over the weekend; nobody gave a shit about the magazine or the state of our jobs.

I didn't last long at *George* (I was John's assistant and John was dead), but before I left, I found myself locked in a battle with the publishing company over my severance. Because my executive assistant title was that of an entry-level position, the Hachette HR wanted to give me six weeks of severance. Meanwhile, editors who were part of the mass exodus after

John's death and who hadn't worked for the magazine nearly as long as I had were getting six months. I might have just taken the money and walked—moved on with my life, even though I felt like I didn't have one—but when Hachette tried to renege half my bonus because I didn't work the whole year, I decided to fight (I eventually won, after John's lawyers got involved).

I stayed through the last issue John had worked on, which we refused to call a tribute because John would have *hated* that. "Oh, brother, people die every day," I could hear him say in my head.

John had said that if *George* ever folded, he wanted the last cover image to be of George Washington in a coffin, a funny swan song. Matt and I pitched the idea, but nobody was on board. So instead (refusing to put anyone's image—especially John's—on the cover), Matt created a beautiful and memorable design in its powerful simplicity: a blurred image of the American flag blowing in the wind. The flag represented *George* and what it stood for—American politics, John's passion. So we did pay tribute to John, in a way that would have made him proud.

The only other magazine whose cover rivaled *George*'s was *The New Yorker,* which published an image of the Statue of Liberty with a black veil over her face. When my issue came in the mail the week after John died, I was touched—I always felt that John wasn't taken seriously enough, and nothing is more serious than *The New Yorker.*

More than a month after John died, I said good-bye to *George* and entered into a stultifying daily routine that began when I woke up around 11:00 a.m. There wasn't much more to it than me sitting on my couch drinking coffee, Diet Snapple, and Diet Coke, punctuated with cigarettes, until my afternoon nap at 2:00 p.m., which slid me into the evening. I didn't bother to shower or get dressed. It was like having the flu—except it went on for months. Once in a while I went out at night. But in the daytime, not a chance. My biggest fear was being out during rush hour or lunchtime. Surrounded by people hurrying to work or home, I was reminded of what I didn't have and I panicked. Whereas once I thought my life was charmed, now it felt cursed.

People frequently told me how well I was handling "the situation." *Really?* I thought. *I don't want to handle it well.* I wanted to scream like a lunatic in the streets. And many times I considered it. The memory of John—his grace under pressure and assertion that the way people act under horrible circumstances is the true mark of their character—was the only reason I kept it together, on the outside at least.

My fantasy that Tony and I would ride off into the sunset together faded shortly after the funerals were over and the paparazzi had moved on to the next story. He comforted me after John's service, and together we attended the one for Carolyn and Lauren in Connecticut.

Later in the summer, when Anthony Radziwill passed away from cancer, we were both invited to the funeral at the house of his mother, Lee, in the Hamptons, where Tony also rented a place. When I called him to make plans, I assumed I would stay with him, since he was already out in Long Island. "Let me see if someone has a room for you," he said, and then never called back.

I knew from that call that our connection was gone, but the weekend of the funeral offered painful proof. I stayed with my dear friend Stephanie, who worked as Matt Berman's assistant, and she drove me to the funeral, where Tony was less than attentive. Having held out hope, I told my friend I didn't need a ride home, so I was forced to find a way back with strangers.

It seemed like everything around me was dead: my career, my love life, my closest friends. And then my dad.

In February 2000, seven months after John and Carolyn, and less than two years after Frank, my dad died of a blood clot that went to his lungs. When Dad passed away, I lost my political sparring partner and the only man who took pride in everything I had accomplished. He'd been in the hospital after breaking his hip and was preparing to return to work. I had spoken to him two hours before he told my mom he couldn't breathe, and then collapsed and died before the paramedics arrived.

"Hi, Dad, how are you?" I asked him on the phone.

"I'm fine. I'm all right."

Our conversation was banal, as are most exchanges with people right before they die. What had John and I talked about— air-conditioning? By now I was accustomed to the absurdity of the mundane words attached to moments of such import.

Death followed me, I was sure of it. I was convinced my mother would pass away if I went out of town and was in a constant state of high alert, wondering who would be next. I read meaning into ordinary occurrences. I found signs everywhere, and they all spelled fatal events for my loved ones.

Yes, I was watchful of everyone—except myself. I didn't care what happened to me. My survival instinct had drowned in all that death. One afternoon, I stepped off a curb on Third Avenue, near my apartment, and began to cross against the light when a bus passed inches away from me. Such a moment should have taken my breath away at the thinness of the line between life and death. But instead of sighing with relief, I felt nothing. *So what if the bus had hit me?*

My mom used to say that "death can't be that bad, because nobody has ever come back." I thought, *If it happens to me, so be it.* I was broken in a way that couldn't be fixed. I would simply have to learn to live with my injury and move forward, even though I was certain that everything good in my life had already happened.

I thought I'd never feel better again, but I couldn't hole up in my apartment forever. I was running through my severance and needed to make money. The offers weren't exactly pouring in, and I didn't know how to look for another job. So I called a headhunting agency that advertised in the *New York Times.* "High-profile executive assistant positions," the advertisement boasted.

I should have realized it was a bad idea. A higher-profile assistant position than the one I had did not exist. What was I going to do—work for the pope? But walking into the headhunter's dingy, gray reception area was worse than I could have imagined. The magazines in the waiting room were depressingly out-of-date. An actress on the cover of *People* boasting about the secret to her happy marriage was now divorced. A *Martha Stewart Living* had 101 ideas for summer entertaining even though we were in the dead of winter. The heavily pawed issues reinforced the cheapness of the midtown office.

I looked out of place in my navy Narciso Rodriguez suit with a skirt that hit tastefully above the knee and a cinched jacket that showed off my tiny waist (the grief diet). To complement the perfect suit, I wore a pair of gorgeous black leather Manolo Blahnik slingbacks with little bows atop the pointy toes. Long before *Sex and the City* had popularized the brand, I wanted a pair but couldn't bring myself to spend five hundred dollars on shoes. When I was leaving *George,* the staff presented me with a thousand-dollar gift certificate to the discreet boutique, hidden away on West 55th Street (Carolyn would have been so proud that I had my first Manolos).

I decided to wear them to the headhunter's office, assuming the better I looked, the better the jobs they would send my way. But like so many other misguided moments I had experienced over the past several months, my outfit was a joke against the backdrop of the run-down space. When I saw "reason for termination of last job" on the form I was to fill out, I couldn't stand it anymore and left.

In the six months since John had passed away, I had trouble figuring out what to do next. I was so confused, I could hardly decide what to eat for lunch (if I ate at all), let alone plan for the rest of my life. I didn't want to work for anyone but John. The trust he had put in me, the relationship we had forged, the work I did for him, all that I had learned—how would I ever find another dream job like that? Selling myself to prospective employers was the last thing I felt prepared to do.

I didn't even feel comfortable putting the name JFK Jr. on my résumé. Still wanting to protect his privacy, I refused to offer the details of my job, no matter how innocuous. But it was the only work I had to show for myself.

So far, however, John's name was only a distraction. People hiring tripped out when they saw it—either asking me to share or, more likely, sharing their own stories. At one job interview, the man reviewing my résumé burst into tears. "I remember where I was when he died," he said, reaching out to hold my hand for support. "My friend called me, and it was so hard because I watched him grow up."

The entire world knew John or, rather, wanted to feel as if they knew him. So anytime I met someone new, whether at an interview or out with a friend, I had to sit through the John Kennedy Jr. Rorschach test. Having been his assistant, I became a convenient receptacle for everyone's reactions—people put him on a pedestal or tore him down. Listening to people tell me what John was really like didn't anger me (if anything it was a comforting reminder of his significant place in time), but it did become tedious.

Occasionally, I became incensed. During an interview for the assistant position to the powerful founder of a big company, the executive spent the entire time asserting his virility over that of a dead man. "This job is going to be the complete opposite of whatever you did before," he said. "I'm not looking to promote myself the way John Kennedy did." Instantly despising him, I wanted to say, "You couldn't promote yourself like John Kennedy if you handed out a million dollars in cash on the street."

The insensitivity of strangers I encountered was unbearable.

"I heard his wife was cheating on him."

"He was so dumb."

"That magazine was failing anyway."

"Why'd he get in that plane?"

We are three months out of this. Can you give me a fucking break? But I didn't lash out because I understood John wasn't real to most people. He was a headline or a photo. So

229

I stopped defending him. Now that he was gone, the effort seemed pointless. Instead, I limited interactions with people I didn't know and went blank when others delivered their John Kennedy dissertations.

So I wound up like any other lost soul, taking a series of random jobs. Without the counsel of John, Carolyn, Frank, or my dad, I bounced from moment to moment as if I were taking a ride on someone else's life.

As a receptionist for a famous photographer, I answered phones, filled the copier with paper, and arranged for the dog walker. Within days I was mind-numbingly bored. My title with John was that of an assistant, but the job had been more like a chief of staff—prioritizing his schedule, organizing his life, keeping the freaks away, offering judgment on important issues. It didn't occur to me until after John died how amazing it was that my opinion had value to someone like him. I'd had a privileged position. And now I was taking messages from massage therapists and professional poop scoopers.

The receptionist gig didn't stick. I turned to catering and freelance PR stints—doing junior-level or menial tasks that, thankfully, didn't require much thought or last too long. The cash tided me over, but whenever I rushed out from the kitchen in a uniform, carrying a platter of mini crab cakes, I worried that I'd see someone from my former life.

It was bound to happen eventually. New York isn't a big place when you travel in certain circles. Stationed outside the new Hermès store on Madison Avenue for an event celebrating the boutique's grand opening, I was working the door, pulling famous people out of the line and ushering them into the store—the kind of job twenty-year-old starry-eyed interns do. I was scanning the line for angry celebs when I felt a tap on my shoulder. I turned around and saw Matt, the pity on his face pure torture. "Is this what it's come to?" he said. "If John were alive right now, he would be like, 'Can someone *please* get that headset off her?'"

If John were alive. I thought those words all the time.

Eventually, I heard about a job I wanted. Word went around in political circles, where I still maintained sources, that Bill Clinton was looking for an assistant for his new, postpresidential offices in Harlem. Although it was another assistant position, I really wanted that job. And I was perfect for it. Aiding a charismatic man with obvious sex appeal and an overabundance of public attention, who everybody wanted a piece of but who also needed to maintain a cogent, smooth, targeted schedule in the most discreet manner—the job had my name written all over it.

I started working the phones like I used to do for John, but now I was making calls on my behalf and the process was not nearly as smooth. My first call was to Senator Kennedy's office. I thought Ted Kennedy might write me a letter of recommendation. Not only had I worked closely with his staff through the engagement rumors, wedding aftermath, and of course, funeral ordeal, but also he knew me personally. He had witnessed my unwavering loyalty to and efforts in support of John on more than a few occasions. *This is a no-brainer,* I thought as I put in my request with his assistant.

But my request was quickly rejected. The senator couldn't call the president's office on my behalf, one of his aides instructed, because that would be asking for a favor. Only once had he done that, for his sister Jean, and he wouldn't be able to do it for me.

I was stunned. I wasn't asking to become secretary of state, just an assistant. After keeping guard for so long, I thought I might have earned a favor. But I learned the hard way that that's not the way politics works. I tracked down my old admirer Harold Ickes, with whom I had shared that enchanted evening at the correspondents' dinner, which now felt like a distant dream. Clinton's former adviser remembered me and happily wrote a lovely note in which he said, "I've never worked with this girl, but she's worth looking at."

I didn't get the job, and I felt like the biggest loser in the world, even though a friend of mine explained that it didn't have anything to do with me. It was the John Kennedy Jr. Complex. "God could have written you a recommendation letter, and it wouldn't have mattered," he said. "There's no way Clinton would let himself be compared to JFK Jr. No guy wants the girl who used to sit outside John's office sitting outside his."

The past five years seemed to count for nothing. No, it was worse than that; it was as if they counted against me. I had gone from being someone who could open any door with the magic words "from John Kennedy's office" to someone who was completely powerless. Tragedy followed me around like a shadow; it was written across my résumé and accompanied me on every outing. I was a different person from the girl who had told John off when he took my office at PR/NY—I knew that much. But I wondered if it was worth the pain of losing it all. Maybe it would have been better if the past five years hadn't happened. Maybe it would've been better if John and I had never met.

CHAPTER
12
——

I stood in the wings of the stage and took one final look at the audience before the show started. As the theater lights dimmed, I could see family and friends fill the seats of the packed house. There was Nancy, my best friend from high school, a college friend who had flown in from Los Angeles, my sisters, Jessica, Matt, and several of my other friends from *George*. And of course, there was my mom: front row and center.

They had all come to support me on the opening night of the off-Broadway play, *Touch,* that I had produced with Michele and another dear friend, Robin Chambers, Robert De Niro's longtime assistant, whom I had met when the actor posed for the cover of *George*. Despite all the hard work I had put in to get to this point, the moment felt like magic.

I first read the script for *Touch* right after John's death in 1999. After the funeral was over and the packing done, I took off for Vermont with Michele to get away and try to clear my head.

A professional actress, Michele had brought along the script about an astronomer whose wife of six happy years goes out to buy whipping cream on Thanksgiving and never comes back. She's later found murdered and buried on a Navajo reservation. When I saw the emotion it elicited in Michele, I decided to read the script. Halfway through, I was sobbing.

The story spoke directly to my own experience. The main character, Kyle, trying to deal with the sudden loss of a loved one, doesn't know how he'll go on. In many respects, he doesn't want to go on. He would rather remain in the past, no matter how painful it is to be there. I felt that way, too. Knowing that you can survive grief takes a long time.

The first few months after John died, I was inundated with beautiful and touching condolence cards, notes, and calls. It was comforting to be in constant contact with John and Carolyn's friends and family members. As long as everyone else was grieving with me, I could hold on to them and the life that I had with them. I didn't have to move on.

Eventually, of course, people moved on. That's when my grief became paralyzing. John's death was all I thought about for the first few years afterward. He had such a lasting impact that all those associated with him ask themselves from time to time, "What would my life be like today if John were still around?" For me the question was ever present. John had been my day-to-day, and so became his absence.

Because I could never replace him or my experience at *George*, I didn't know what to do. I had to get a sense of who I was without being associated with the most famous person in the world. As I struggled to forge a new identity and reinvent my career, bringing *Touch* to the stage became a labor of love. I wasn't a theater producer, but with Michele and Robin equally enthusiastic about the project, I was sure we could make it happen. I wanted to see Kyle come alive.

In 2000, with the playwright Toni Press-Coffman's blessing, we sent the script to nonprofit theaters throughout the city, but we received "don't call us, we'll call you" responses. I couldn't believe they didn't see the clear genius of the play. Michele, Robin, and I never gave up (although sometimes, while waiting forever at Tower Copy East for the copies to be done, we wanted to). We continued to check in with theaters and send the script out to new ones until, two years later, someone finally bit. The Women's Project, a twenty-five-year-old all-female theater company, included *Touch* in a reading that went so well, they decided to mount the show in the fall of 2003 with Michele as Kathleen, the prostitute who develops a complicated relationship with Kyle, played by Tom Everett Scott.

Michele called me at 5:30 a.m. the day the *New York Times* reviewed our play; they called it a "gripping, heart-wrenching, tender drama." I was ecstatic, and not just because the *Times* and audiences loved the show. Achieving the near-impossible dream of mounting a play in New York City was a turning point for me, bringing me out of grief and back into life. The *Times* could have been talking about me when it described Kyle as emerging "at the end with a weight that will never lighten but with his sense of wonder and possibility intact."

I would never forget John. But the production of *Touch* was the first time in years that I had accomplished something that had nothing to do with working for him. With the help of friends and family, *Touch* was my achievement.

It was a funny contradiction. If I had never worked for John

Kennedy, becoming more sophisticated through the prestige and the perks and earning respect in a demanding role, I would never have dared to produce a play. But if I had continued to work for him, I probably wouldn't have done it, either. Life with John and Carolyn was wonderful but all-consuming. They were the center of my life, and once they were gone, I had to fill that place myself.

Just as with producing *Touch,* I could never have imagined owning my own business while I worked for John (I had planned to stay by his side no matter where he went, even to the White House). After he died, no one I could possibly have worked for was equal to him (other than, perhaps, the president, but he wasn't hiring). So, eventually, I decided to work for me.

With the help of my mentor, Nancy Haberman, I returned to my PR roots in 2004 and launched my own firm, RMT PR Management. Working out of a cozy office in Chelsea, I began with a few top-notch clients such as Richie Notar from Nobu and the political commentators James Carville and Paul Begala. I had John to thank for more than just helping me land big names out of the gate. To this day, I continue to use the lessons John taught me. Whether I'm helping a client weather a public crisis or trying to drum up more business, I aim to be appropriate, restrained, and fair. My motto is "underpromise and overdeliver." In my business, people get hired because they promise a client an appearance on the *Today* show within a month. But when they can't produce, they just get fired. John believed in being honest and up-front with people, and so do I.

His example is one reason I'm able to remain gracious (for the most part) even in pressure-filled situations. The other reason is my mother. She believed in me and felt I deserved success, even when I was at my lowest. The frustration she showed when I was a kid, about her own life, turned into a passion for me to have the best life possible. On the opening night of *Touch,* she didn't stop smiling the entire evening. When I got home, there was a message from her on my answering machine.

"RoseMarie, it's your mother [as if I didn't know]. I am so proud of you, and your father would have been so proud, too. You are such an amazing woman and I love you very much."

After my father passed away, I worried about her living alone. So I was grateful that because I owned a PR firm, I could occasionally work from her house and had the freedom to spend more time helping her out. (She refused to hire a cleaning lady until her dying day, and I would find her, at eighty years old, standing on a ladder washing the windows.)

Maybe it was my mother's unwavering faith in me that made her death so devastating. Or maybe it was that I had lost so many people—Frank, John, Carolyn, and my dad—within a matter of several years. Or maybe it was just that she was my mom. But in 2006, right after Thanksgiving, she collapsed while visiting my sister in Florida. Arriving at the hospital to see my mother on life support and looking nothing like herself, I have never experienced such fear and intense sadness. I kept a vigil at her bedside and slept on a couch in the waiting room. I felt like I was ten years old and couldn't leave my mother for even a minute. "Please, Mom, don't leave me," I begged her. "I can't live if you're not here. Please, wake up. I will do anything if you would just wake up. Please."

By the fourth day, all hope was gone. We took her off life support, and I spent the next twelve hours at her side, watching her chest go up and down until it stopped. We buried my mother three weeks before the most brutal Christmas ever. I had felt alone before, but without my mother, the person who went to sleep at night wondering if I was okay, the world felt empty.

A few weeks later, while my sisters and I were cleaning out her house, I came across four large brown envelopes marked ANITA, ANDREA, AMY, and ROSEMARIE. Inside each one were pieces of her jewelry and a note.

To Rose Marie

You are my shining star. Even though you were the youngest you amazed me for your good sense and charisma. When there was a problem or a question you were the word of wisdom and you emerged with a solution. God bless you and keep you. I love you with all my heart
Love.
Mom.

I knew my mother loved me, but I never realized how much she admired me. When I put myself down as simply a girl from the Bronx who was lucky enough to meet JFK Jr. and win his trust, she knew better. While I owed John a lot, I didn't owe him everything. He and I were similar: we valued loyalty, intelligence, and determination, and those qualities were more significant than the superficial traits that set us apart. They allowed me to do my job well for John and continued to push me forward in spite of the ordinary disappointment and sorrow that accompanies any life.

The greatest tragedy of life is that at some point we have

to say good-bye to the people we've spent a lifetime loving, whether it's John Kennedy or Marion Terenzio. Religion. Therapy. There's no good answer to it. Death just doesn't make sense. And there's no antidote to the emptiness it leaves in its wake. You don't forget the dead even though they can no longer console you, inspire you, or make you laugh.

I often wonder what John would have thought of this or that news event or political headline, and so many times, I imagine what he'd say if I shouted over to him from the desk in my office to ask his advice on a PR decision. When I do something stupid, it makes me laugh to think how he would have made fun of me for it.

Standing in front of the mirror, I sometimes ask myself, "Would Carolyn be caught dead in this?" If the answer is no, the outfit immediately comes off. Same with guys I'm dating. If they don't meet Carolyn's standards, they don't meet mine, either.

I wished Frank had been there to help me through the loss of John, my parents, and, paradoxically, his own death. But whenever I attend a fabulous party, take a luxurious trip, or eat at an amazing restaurant, I enjoy it for both of us.

When the latest political scandal makes headlines, I can hear my father saying, "Another arrogant son of a bitch." I would give anything to sit with him on election night and fight over the outcome. And although I miss my mother so much it feels like there is a hole in my chest, I take out her letter and read it now and then as a testament to and reminder of my best self.

When it comes to death, you don't get over it; you just get on with it. Like with Christmas. A year after my mom died, I panicked in the months before the holidays. Those big gatherings were some of the best moments with my family. I missed cooking with my mother late into the night before Christmas Eve and sitting around a huge table with twenty other people, laughing, drinking, eating, and, of course, arguing. Now I had to make my own plans.

Instead of visiting my sisters, who were each celebrating with their own families, I decided to rent a house outside the city and invite friends. I found a beautiful farmhouse with horses and wild turkeys running around outside and enough bedrooms to sleep anyone who wanted to come. The tight-knit group that I share most of my life with—including Nick, a six-foot-two Australian charmer who calls me Rack (for reasons only those who know me will understand); my travel buddy and *George* alum, Scott, and his sister Brooke; Joey and Paul, friends from my college days who often accompanied Frank and me on our adventures; my friend Liz, whom Matt refers to as Diana Vreeland; Libby, who works side by side with me every day to build my business, and her sister Kirby; Meghan and Jim, whom I met through Libby; and of course, Michele—helped me fill the house. I also invited anyone else who didn't have a place to go—including my office IT guy.

When I was growing up, every holiday would find some stranger at our table. Sometimes it was my mom's coworker who wore odd hats with feathers sticking out or fake roses around the brim. Other times it was an Argentine named Chi Chi with fire-engine-red hair. My sisters and I complained, "Who's *this* person?" And my mom's answer was always the same: "Never mind who it is. No one should be alone on a holiday."

The best part of the house I rented upstate was the kitchen, which we lived in that entire holiday. (The only time we weren't in there was when we were in bed.) It was huge, with a farmhouse table that could comfortably seat twenty, a couch, an island, two massive ovens, a six-burner stove, and windows on three full walls. I was in heaven, cooking while surrounded by everyone else listening to music, playing cards, and talking. I made everything from scratch and prepared some of my mom's classic recipes. Memories flooded back with the smell of my mother's meatballs and homemade apple pie, and as they mixed with the scents of dishes from my friends' traditions, I was grateful for this warm reinvention of holidays, family, and celebration.

As I took a sip of wine and looked at the beautiful tree we had decorated the night before, images of earlier Christmases ran through my mind: the heaps of gifts from Carolyn, teasing John about his carriage ride up Fifth Avenue, my mother and father bickering over ornaments, Frank's place around our table.

I still think about the past and the people who filled it, but I no longer dwell on what might have been. It's enough of a struggle finding the light at the end of the tunnel and knowing that eventually you'll come out the other side. You can't mourn the dead forever. Don't glamorize them or demonize them, either. As John used to say, life is for the living.

ACKNOWLEDGMENTS

———

Thank you to Steve Troha for taking a chance on me and for giving my story a happily-ever-after. You are my friend, my advisor, and my agent. I could never have done this without you because of how much I trust and respect you.

You can't write a memoir until you find your voice, and Rebecca Paley helped me find my voice and brought my story to life in a way I couldn't have imagined possible. She brought out the best stories I could tell and gave me a safe haven to tell them. You are an amazing collaborator.

The minute I walked into our first meeting, I fell in love with Jen Bergstrom and Trish Boczkowski at Gallery Books. They spoke my language right away, and I prayed so hard that they would take on my story. I am so thrilled to have such an amazing team behind me. Trish took my words and made them stronger and became a dear friend. Jen Bergstrom understood my story and how I wanted it told. Jen Robinson made sure that my story was heard. The rest of the team—my publisher Louise Burke, Kate Dresser, Alex Lewis, Elisa Rivlin, and Steve Breslin—

have been incredible to work with and have made the process so enjoyable.

I am so blessed to have family and friends who have been so supportive and loving. You have all made the best times amazing and the worst times bearable.

I could never have accomplished what I have without Libby Schmitz. Thank you, Libby, for being my champion and for being there every day. I'm so grateful for your encouragement, loyalty, support, and most of all for your friendship.

You can be blasé about some things, Matt Berman, but you are the FIRST person I want to talk to in the morning and the LAST person I want to talk to at night. Your wisdom, savvy, and genius sense of humor have been my greatest strength through all of this. Your friendship and your advice mean the world to me. But 234, this is boring. Turn the lights down and call me later.

My sister Amy Terenzio Schreibman has been my rock, my friend, and my guardian angel. Thank you for holding my hand my whole life and for helping me to realize that everything good is not in the past. You never judged me, and you believed in me when I couldn't bear to believe in myself. Thank you for sharing the best and for getting me through the worst. Thank you to Noah, Joseph, and David Schreibman for all your love and support while I wrote this book.

When I thought my fairy tale was over, Michele Ammon helped me restart it. I am forever grateful for that, and I look forward to every new adventure with you. You are an incredibly kind and generous person and such a wonderful friend.

When I needed John Kennedy's voice in my head, I was lucky to have Brian Steel. Thank you for championing this book. YOU are the real sexiest man alive and have encouraged me to tell my story for so long. Thank you for your loyalty, support, and friendship, and most of all for helping me avoid being harassed.

I am so lucky to have Tricia Viola Woody as my friend. You have been such a force in my life and helped me stand up for myself when I didn't think I could. Meep.

I have had some of the best times of my life with Joey Valentino. You have helped make me who I am today. You have been my family, and I am so grateful for your encouragement and support. Thank you for sticking by me for all of these years and for contributing so much to my life.

I know I can tell Paul Lekakis anything and never be judged. Mouse, your love and support have meant so much to me. Your honesty, bravery, and creative life have been an inspiration to me in all that I do.

When I've needed empathy, support, and someone to really listen, Liz Lalumia has been there for me. You are my dear friend, and you always give it to me straight with or without wine.

I would never have done this book without Jessica Weinstein's approval. You have been Carolyn Bessette Kennedy's voice in my head, and your guidance and support have made this story possible. I'm so grateful for our friendship.

I'm looking forward to sharing a bright and hopeful future with my friend Stephanie Mack. Thank you for all you and your family have done for me all these years and for encouraging me to write this book. Oh, and, "Weeeessss, your Mommy called."

I am so grateful for Scott Schaiberger's support. You're almost as sexy as I am, and I cannot think of anyone better to have as a travel companion. We're getting a facility, Shanique.

Acknowledgments

Since I was thirteen years old, I've had Nancy Olear as my friend. You have been my family, and I treasure all of our memories and look forward to making new ones.

My mentor and friend Nancy Haberman has taught me so much and given me confidence in myself personally and professionally. Your guidance has always led me to do the right thing.

The rack will belong to Nick Mason someday. You make me feel smart and beautiful, and a girl could not ask for more than that.

With gratitude for your guidance, patience, and friendship, Chris Cuomo, you helped me make my story the best it could be. You always make me less sad, and I'm glad you're in the world. Meet the new boss.

My dear friend and fellow Howard Stern fan, Gary Mason. Thank you for your friendship and for all of your support. Hi, Hiney.

When I had doubts about what I was doing, Gary Ginsberg was supportive and encouraging. Thank you for all of your teasing and for your friendship. You can be my Chief of Staff anytime.

My sisters Anita and Andrea, thank you for helping to raise me. When Mom and Dad couldn't always take care of me, you stepped in and helped make me the person I am today.

I'm grateful for the love and support of Barbara Giordano (Mrs. G) and Donna Giordano. Thank you for giving me the gift of Frank and for taking me in as part of your family.

With respect and admiration for Franklin Baez. You have challenged and enhanced my body, mind, and soul.

My *George* alum and my friend, Jeff Sklar. You are a wartime consigliere.

Acknowledgments

To my *George* comrades who helped make my story possible and for all of the good times we've shared: Negi Darsses, Matthew Cowen, Biz Mitchell, Sudie Redmond, Carl Robbins, Sasha Issenberg, Sean Neary, and Michael Berman.

Thank you to Robin Chambers, who has always been the voice of reason.

I have to acknowledge the fierce and fantastic women in my life: Shannon Malone, Katy Hawley, Natalie Hodan, Brooke Schaiberger, Kirby Schmitz, Hillary Rivman, Deb Elko, Erica Salvatore, Robin Renzi, Jenny Schmitz, Susannah Cahalan, and Laura Fink.

For encouraging me to tell my story for so long and for being the best crooner ever, thank you to Steven Santagati.

Thank you to Steve Friedman, A.J. Benza, Gary Dell'Abate, Ron Wilde, J.D. Shapiro, Dr. Stephen Nicholas, and Eric Hyman.